Published by: Les Cowie Consulting, LLC

Versions: eBook Paperback - also Kindle - Color

Manufactured in the United States of America

Library of Congress Cataloging-in-Publication Data

Cowie, Les

ISBN-13: 978-0991022328
ISBN-10: 0991022327
LCCN: 2017914441
BISAC: BUS097000 BUSINESS & ECONOMICS / Workplace Culture
BISAC: BUS059000 BUSINESS & ECONOMICS / Skills
Les Cowie Consulting, LLC, Maitland, FL

Title: New Job? – Fast Start! 7 Steps to be seen mastering your new job quickly.

Website: www.7stepslms.com

Facebook: New Job? Fast Start

Graphics by: Olivia De Alba, Orlando, Florida.
Animations by: Jamori Montgomery, Orlando, Florida.
(A few elements in the graphics used images designed by Macrovector/Freepik.
 See: www.freepik.com.)

Website by Hive Media Studio - hivemediastudio.com

7 Step Software by TechieAid - https://techieaid.in/

Pictures: Some pictures from Google Images.

Acknowledgments

I wish to thank my wife, Fran, who has been at my side through success and failure. For more than 48 years, she lovingly and compassionately stood by me through many challenging times. She believed in me, supported me, and was my companion and best friend through all these years. She is also my hero having fought colon and liver cancer with grace and dignity. Fran passed on March 8, 2017 but she is still a big part of my life in Spirit. She has inspired every good thing I have done in my life.

I wish to acknowledge the support and encouragement of our children, Rob (best known as the Producer of the movie: "The Blair Witch Project"), our daughter, Colette, a remarkable expert in motherhood and Internet marketing, and our son, Ian, a young entrepreneur stepping out with his first company.

I need to thank the many additional people who read the drafts of this book and generously contributed comments and edits, including: Kelly Bryan, Ian Darwent, David Foret, Patrick Jansson (Sweden), Marney Kaye, Colette Marshall, Sue Montgomery (UK), Jonathan Moore, Lynn Nelson, Janet Riley, Mike Stewart, Richard Ungaro, and Richard Welton (Australia).

I wish to acknowledge the outstanding technical work of Kiran Gopalakrishna and Sudhir Gurjar of TechieAid, India who developed the 7 Steps Master application and the apps for the Apple Store and Google Play: https://techieaid.in/

I so appreciate the help of Kelley Wilson and Sarah Cowie of Hive Media Studios for the design and content of the 7 Steps website. hivemediastudio.com

I am grateful for the efforts of Mike Stewart of sales@websitesyoucontrolyourself.com for his assistance with epublishing, web development, podcast development and Internet marketing.

So now to help people make significant strides in new jobs and preparing to move up the organization ladder quickly.

About "New Job? Fast Start!"

Be seen mastering your new job quickly. Whether you are a Talent Developer or an employee in a job, when you've applied the 7 Steps ™ we recommend in this book, you'll rapidly master the content of any new job. You will know the 20% of activities that will occur 80% of the time and the 20% of faults that may occur 80% of the time. You will know with whom you should build relationships to be effective and successful in the job. You will be able to capture all the content of a new job using the 7 Steps software application and then make the content available for you and others doing the same job. You will have prepared yourself to be upwardly mobile in your new company. You will be prepared to succeed.

About the Author

Les Cowie has enjoyed a distinguished career working with venture capital groups and organizations in the USA over the last 27 years. He has been involved in the acquisition and development of medium to large businesses including manufacturing, commercial and service enterprises. This has led either to a successful sale of the business or to an IPO on US stock exchanges. In every case, the subsequent success of the business has depended on strict attention to process improvements and talent development. Les developed a practical methodology for organizational trainers to follow which helps them quickly analyze critical occupations, determine the minimum necessary training content required for initial talent development and deliver instruction through a combination of web-based videos and simple job-related simulators available to prospective employees via computer, digital pads or smart phones. The approach changes the role of instructors from being 'talking heads' to productivity *coaches*. While there is nothing new about the learning technologies and techniques he advocates, his combination and sequence for the occupation developer's process is innovative and down-to-earth.

Foreword

Richard Ungaro
CEO – RU Investment, LLC Orlando, FL eMail: 4Ungaro@gmail.com

"Most of my professional career has been spent with very successful, high-growth companies. To support a quality growth rate, a company must attract and develop the most talented candidates and prepare them for future leadership roles to sustain that high-growth rate.

This book would have been mandatory reading in all those high-growth companies because it clearly outlines the importance of personal development to meet the future leadership needs of the organization. If you are starting a new job, the information in this book is important for you to read and comprehend because the material will help you be known as a self-starter and a potential rising-star within your department and ultimately your company.

If you are not starting a new job, the information in this book can be a road map to helping you stand out among your peers by demonstrating your initiative, adaptability and "added value" to the company leadership resulting in a more rapid progression through your company's structure."

Rich Ungaro has an extensive 40-year career as a Senior Executive with a special focus on turnarounds, differentiating brands and exponential growth that leads to sustainable competitive advantage.

Rich began his career with Burger King Corporation, as an Project Engineer in the Research & Development Department. He later became their first Vice President of Architecture and Construction and ended his 10-year service as Company/Franchise Operations Manager. He also spent 9-years with Wendy's International in a variety of leadership roles, including Senior Vice President of Operations in the US and Chairman for Wendy's of Canada. During those 9-years, Wendy's grew from 900 restaurants to over 4,000 while opening as many as 500 new stores per year. From 1990 to 1997, Rich served a variety of executive positions with Blockbuster Entertainment Group while the company grew from 900 retail stores to 6,500 never opening less than 700 new stores per year. His last assignment was Executive Vice President for all 6,500 domestic retail stores. Rich also served as Zone Vice President for Starbucks Coffee Company when the company only had 9 retail stores open within the East Coast markets and 250-retail stores nationally. Within 24-months, the East Coast team opened 150-new retail stores at a rate of one new market each month.

CHAPTER 1   CAPTURING AND DELIVERING JOB CONTENT   9

Distributed and Simultaneous Capture of Job Content   9

The 7 Steps Application   12

On Demand Look Up   13

Packaged Learning   14

Development for Delivering the Learning Experience   15

Blank Worksheets for Information Capture   15

CHAPTER 2   THE 7 STEPS   16

Environments   16
    Internal Environment   16
    External Environment   17

Flow   18

INs and OUTs   19

Frequency   21

Checklists   22

Faults   23

Patrolling   24

Summary of the 7 Steps   26

CHAPTER 3   WHAT'S THE JOB ENVIRONMENT   27

Internal Environment   27
    Things to Do and Questions to Ask to Determine the Job's Internal Environment   30

External Environment   32
    Things to Do and Questions to Ask to Determine the Job's External Environment   33

Why Capture and Diagram the Environments?   33

CHAPTER 4   WHAT'S THE FLOW IN THE JOB?   35

Process Flow for a Supermarket Cashier   35
    Things to Do and Questions to Ask to Determine the Job's Process Flow   37

CHAPTER 5   INS AND OUTS   **39**

The Job Description   **39**

Feed Forward and Feedback   **41**
Restaurant Server – INs and OUTs with Controls   44
Things to Do' and 'Questions to Ask' to List "Outs", "Ins", "Processes", and "Controls"   46
'Questions to Ask   46

CHAPTER 6   FREQUENCIES IN THE JOB   **49**

The Pareto Principle   **49**
Things to Do and Questions to Ask Exploring Frequencies in Job Content   51

CHAPTER 7   CHECKLISTS   **53**
Things to Do and Questions to ask to review Checklists   54

CHAPTER 8   FAULTS   **57**

Key Elements in Fault Identification and Correction   **57**
Fault Analysis   57
Fault Frequencies   58
Fault Details Capture   58
Fault Diagnosis and Correction Display Layout   59
Fault Checklists   60
Things to Do and Questions to ask to build Fault Checklists   60

CHAPTER 9   PATROLLING   **63**

Example of a Patrol Pattern When Driving   **63**

Developing a Patrol Pattern and Inspection Sequence   **64**

Sensory Elements in a Patrol Pattern   **64**

Example 1 - Patrol Pattern with Movement   **64**

Example 2 - Patrol Pattern – Close Up   **67**

Benefits of Different Patrol Patterns   **67**

Impact of Frequencies in Developing Your Patrol Pattern   **70**
Things to Do and Questions to ask to build a Patrol Pattern and Inspection Sequence   70

CHAPTER 10   TIPS FOR YOUR FIRST WEEK IN THE NEW JOB   **73**

Day 1   **73**
Things to Do and Questions to Ask in the First Few Days in the New Job   73

CHAPTER 11   MOVING UP   **77**

Reaching Out from Day 1   77

Build the Job Masterfile   77

Importance of the Job Masterfile   77

Moving Up to the Next Job   78

People who have been Successful Using these 7 Steps   79

Be Successful   80

SUPPLEMENTAL READING   **81**
- Do an Internet search for "Scholarly articles for Systems theory in learning"   81
- Do an Internet Search on "Scholarly articles for learning theory psychology"   81

INDICES   **82**

TABLE OF FIGURES   **83**

CHAPTER 1   CAPTURING AND DELIVERING JOB CONTENT

So you're an individual Talent Developer in a corporation or you're a person newly assigned to solve a training challenge in your organization. Or, awesome, you've have landed a new job. Or perhaps you are a manager who wants to accelerate the rate at which your new employees become productive.

Do you want to make favorable impressions quickly? Do you have an action plan for how to understand what will make you successful?

This book offers seven simple tools to accelerate the time between starting to analyze a job and being in command of the content. It's important to encourage an employee who is new to a job to reach out and not wait for someone to take them by the hand.

The 7 Steps Process is like taking an X-ray view of the job from seven different angles. Even if a new employee is moving into a position similar to one held in another company, your company has its differences. Most companies have their unique cultural and procedural differences.

Whether you're a learning experience developer or an employee, if you use these 7 Steps and apply them carefully, you'll be able to focus on the critical elements in the job with the correct perspective.

Let us start by summarizing the seven elements that are common to ALL jobs. When you agree that these elements will apply to that new job, you'll soon see how you can capture information about the job just by asking the right questions and getting answers from the right people. This book introduces you to a computer application that will help you capture all the content needed to be successful in the job. It explains how you will be able to upload and assemble documents, images, pictures, signage, regulations, forms and procedures – even videos recorded with the help of a video camera or your smartphone or smartpad – everything in one place.

7 Steps has been designed for international use. The initial release allows switching from English to French, German, Spanish and Portuguese. (Figures 1 and 2.) Other language translations are in process.

Distributed and Simultaneous Capture of Job Content

Every corporation is challenged to provide quality learning experiences for multiple jobs. The challenge is how to do this quickly to build and develop the organization to optimum levels of success as quickly and economically as possible. Using the 7 Steps software application allows a corporation to distribute the task of capturing job content over a broader base of contributors than just a few Talent Developers and Organization Developers. The application opens the opportunity for multiple job experts to capture content for subsequent processing by Learning Experience Developers and Organization Developers. This is where you can play an important role.

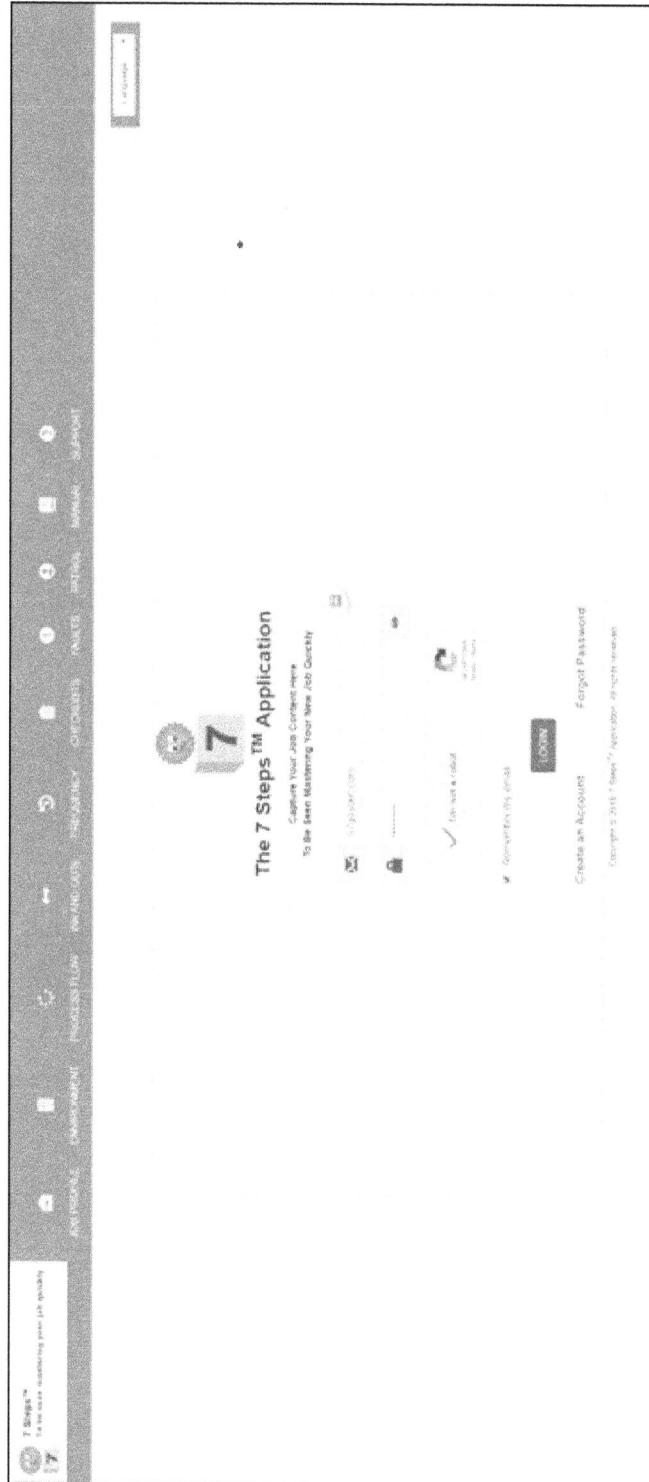

Figure 1 English Log-in for 7 Steps

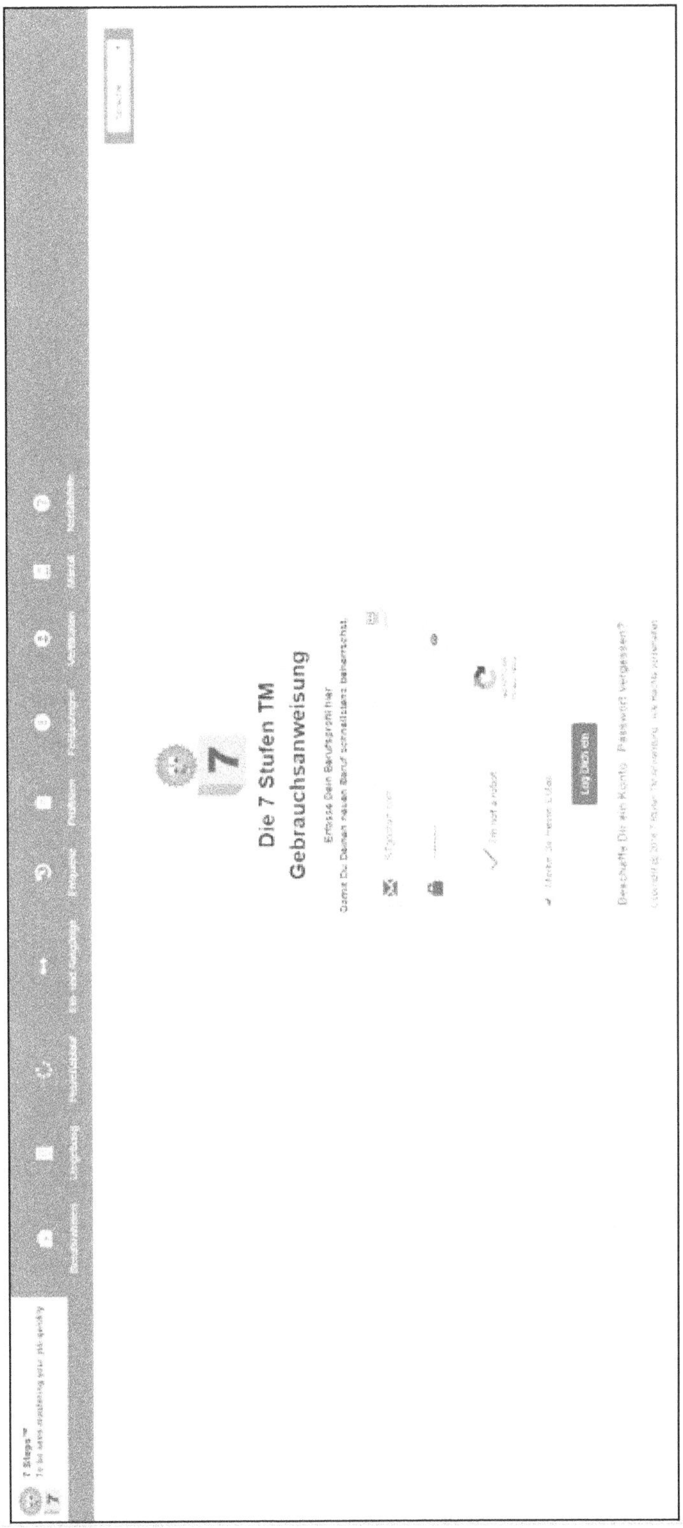

Figure 2 Multi-Language Log-in for 7 Steps

The 7 Steps Application

The 7 Steps application is a system for researching job content, capturing all necessary information related to performing the job, and then delivering appropriate learning experiences to employees via a computer, smartphone, smartpad or even a virtual reality headset. The 7 Steps application facilitates the development of a corporate library of occupations – an in-house 'Jobflix'.

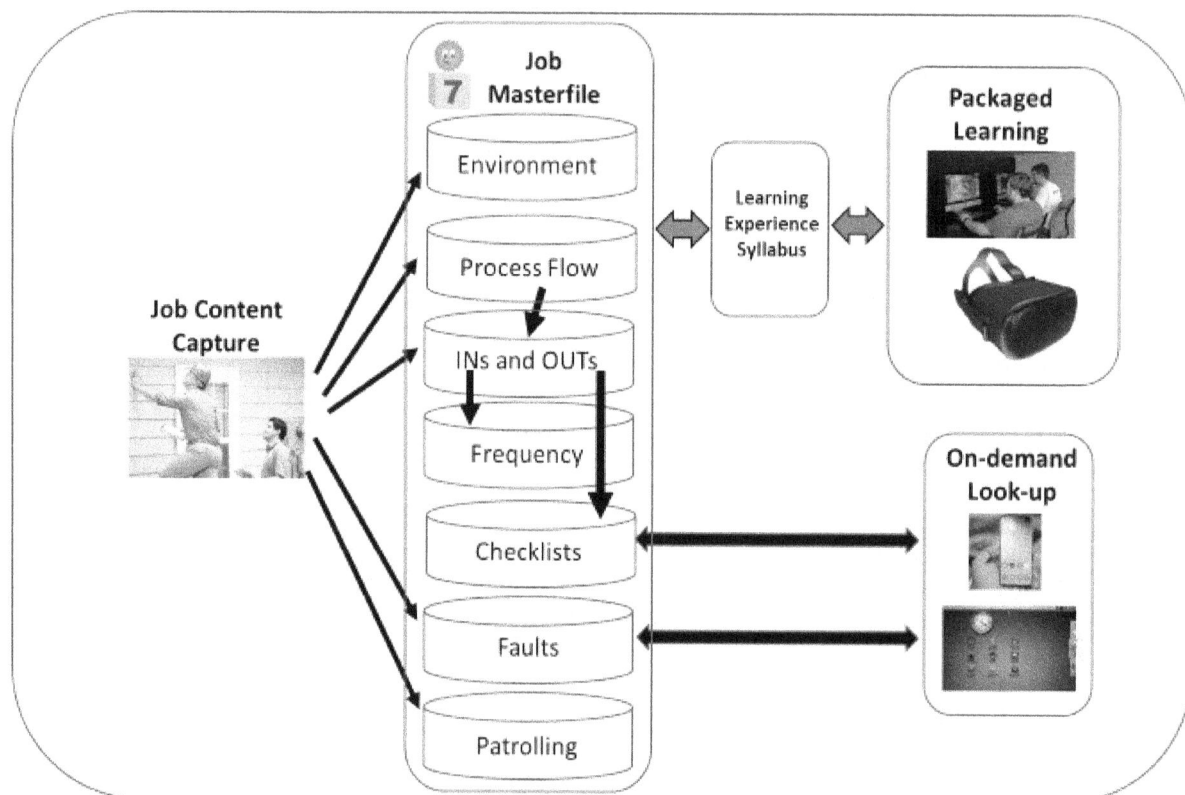

Figure 3 Using the 7 Steps System to best benefit

An occupation Researcher, whether an experienced Talent Developer, a job expert under the supervision of a 7 Step trained mentor, or you as a new employee asking the right questions. uses the 7 Step application to capture the content of a selected occupation. (Figure 3.) 7 Steps creates a "Masterfile" of all the job content in each of the 7 Steps from "Environment" to "Patrolling". As an occupation Researcher, not only can you capture text content, you can upload, and store videos captured on video cameras, smartphones or smartpads. You can upload images, pictures, critical documents, safety signage and procedures – examples of everything an employee on the job may encounter and need to use. 7 Steps is 'everything for a job - in one place.

Once you have captured and diagramed the Internal and External Environments, the Process Flow and the INs and OUTs for each step in the Process Flow, the 7 Steps application generates the content for the analysis of frequencies to determine the 20% that happens 80% of the time. It also generates the Checklists tabling the required task sequences and Best Practices.

You then capture all the information needed for accurate Fault Diagnosis and Correction. 7 Steps also allows Researchers to secure the recommended Best Practice versions of the Patrol Patterns and Inspection Sequences to use for excellent performance on-the-job.

You will then be able to determine how best to deliver this content to existing employees and new job entrants. The options are:

- Access the job content on-demand from any location with access to the Internet.
- A detailed "Packaged Learning Experience" with teaching and testing.
- Both

On Demand Look Up

Current technologies allow the delivery of required information to an employee as they need it. Once the content of a job has been captured through the 7 Step process, the 7 Steps applications in the Apple Store and Google Play can be used by employees to look up checklists, including videos and other job content, or get help with Fault Diagnosis and Correction on-demand at the tap of an icon.

The difference between this approach and the 'Packaged Learning' approach is one of complexity and cost.

In the 'Packaged Learning' approach, the video content is typically professionally planned, scheduled, recorded, edited, packaged and then delivered. In the 'On Demand' approach, a learning experience developer – or an employee with (or without) job experience – can capture short video clips on a smartphone or smartpad without professional production and link these to individual steps in the checklist for an employee to access and view on-demand.

This can be done without having to use professional lighting, editing and narration. The narration may be provided by the employee being recording as the job is executed correctly. Mentors, supervisors, managers, quality and safety experts can view the mini-clips and require them to be recaptured if necessary.

7 Steps support will also set up the links to the 7 Steps smartphone/smartpad/computer viewing apps. There are two such apps. One allows a mentor/Talent Developer to access ALL the content captured in the 7 Steps master for an occupation. This allows viewing for all content from Environments to Patrol Pattern and Inspection Sequence. Editing is done on a computer.

For employees who need to view only the Checklists and Fault Diagnosis and Correction procedures from a smartphone or smartpad while working on the job, 7 Steps provides a viewing application that can be downloaded from the Apple Store and Google Play that allows employees to access the information they need.

Packaged Learning

There are different layers of packaged learning. To name a few…

- It may be as simple as a PowerPoint-type presentation requiring delivery by an instructor.
- It may be a recorded presentation delivered via an LMS (Learning Management System)
- It may be a multi-module 2-D recorded video with teaching and testing delivered via the Internet to computers, smartpads and smartphones.
- It may be a virtual reality 3-D recorded video class with teaching and testing delivered via the Internet to virtual reality headsets.

A 'Packaged' Program requires a syllabus, content structure, scripting, and presentation layout. Where 2D, 3D or virtual delivery will be involved it becomes more complex. The 7 Steps application provides the ability to create the syllabus/curriculum.

In practice we have found that the 'Packaged Learning' approach may be applied to 20%, or less, of the jobs in an organization. 'Packaged Learning' is typically required for jobs where:

- There are many employees performing the same task in a single location or geographically different locations.
- Effective customer interaction is critical for sales, customer retention and customer delight.
- Safety is a critical consideration - especially if there is the risk of injury or death
- Quality is a critical consideration
- Cost control is a critical consideration

If you are an employee with Talent Development responsibilities, before starting to research an occupation and capture job content, you should:

1. Compile a list of the in-company jobs most needing productivity improvement.
2. Identify those that are critical from a safety, customer relations, productivity, or cost point of view.
3. Identify which jobs require the right delivery mechanism, for example:
    a. A critical job or safety protocol where employees will benefit best from delivery via 3D virtual reality headsets
    b. Smartphone/smartpad delivery allowing employees to reference Checklists and Fault Diagnosis and Correction procedures on-demand when needed on-the-job.
4. Determine which employee (or employees) should be invited to contribute to capturing content for a particular occupation they know well.
5. Establish a Project Plan to ensure participants:
    a. Communicate the intent of each assignment to other associated employees
    b. Ensure optimum support for the employee undertaking the 7 Step research
    c. Set a target timeline for completion
    d. Ensure that the appointed Researcher receives orientation and training in the 7 Step approach.

Development for Delivering the Learning Experience

If you will be responsible for making this content available to other employees, once the job content you capture has been reviewed and approved by the right authorities in your organization (Supervision, management, quality, safety and employee representatives) you will need agreement on the appropriate delivery format for the learning experience. The questions to be asked and reviewed are:

1. How critical is this occupation's output to customer satisfaction, productivity and safety?
2. How many people require this learning content?
3. How geographically spread are the employees needing this learning?
4. Does the learning experience require remote learning or centralized learning?
5. Does the learning require technical elements like: equipment, materials, components, tools, etc.?
6. Can any of the learning experiences use simulation in place of real technical elements?
7. How much hands-on experience is absolutely necessary?
8. Does the learning experience require a 3D virtual reality experience?
9. Can the employee achieve adequate learning from a 2D video experience?
10. Does the job content require personal job coaching?
11. Can the job be correctly learned by reading only?
12. Can self-learning for this occupation be monitored and evaluated? How?

One of the important goals of each appointed job Researcher is to produce an easily updatable digital Masterfile that allows quick viewing access and even printing of an up-to-date job manual.

Blank Worksheets for Information Capture

For those job Researchers who still prefer to make notes before capturing content in a computer system, 7 Steps provides worksheets that can be obtained from the www.7stepslms.com website. Each worksheet provides blank space on the front page for a diagram or answers. The suggested "Things to Do" and "Questions to Ask" are listed on the back of the page.

The questions we provide will help Researchers to get each interviewee focused on answering in a specific way. However, the information does not always come out in the most logical fashion. Some people are not good teachers. When this happens, Researchers need to capture what they can while the interviewees are talking. Researchers in such a situation should make their notes and then later transfer the information into the correct sections in the 7 Step application. This way the Researcher will capture the critical job content over time although not necessarily in the easy logical sequence set out in the 7 Steps application and worksheets.

CHAPTER 2   THE 7 STEPS

There are seven elements that are common to ALL jobs. When you agree that these elements will apply to any job, you'll soon see how one can capture information about each job just by asking the right questions from the right people. The information, images, videos, documentation, signage – everything impacting the occupation – can be captured in the 7 Steps software application. This book is a guide to you in the role of an Occupation Researcher and Learning Experience Developer.

To help you, we'll initially provide examples of the 7 Step approach as applied to two jobs we all know something about – a Cashier in a supermarket and a Server in a restaurant. We'll also provide the typical "Things to Do" and "Questions to Ask" for each of the 7 Steps for project participants to use to get others talking about the job. This will help them quickly build the seven X-ray views of the job.

So, what's common to every job? It's as easy as:

1. Environments
2. Flow
3. INs and OUTs
4. Frequency
5. Checklists
6. Faults, and
7. Patrolling

Environments

Step 1: Define the job's environments. Every job operates within definable environments. You can describe these as *internal* and *external* environments.

Internal Environment

The Internal Environment is the **space** where the job happens. We define the internal environment by all the 'things' that are within that 'unique' space. These things can include: equipment, furniture, utilities, appliances, electronics, books, computer applications, paperwork and signage used in that 'definable space'. The **space** may be an office, a workshop, a floor space (as in retail or restaurant), even a cockpit (as in the case of a pilot or vehicle driver). As simple as it might sound, one of the Researcher's first tasks should be to establish "What's the space in which the job must function? What are the people and things in that space the employee will interact with to perform the job?"

External Environment

Every job has its own definable *external* environment. In most cases, this relates to how the employee should interact with other people outside of the immediate workspace. It includes how the employee relates to departments and facilities both within your organization and outside of the organization. Plotting the *external* environment requires an understanding of all the relevant interactions the job requires and how much time is typically spent interacting with other departments, functions, or people. Each employee will interact with some people more than others.

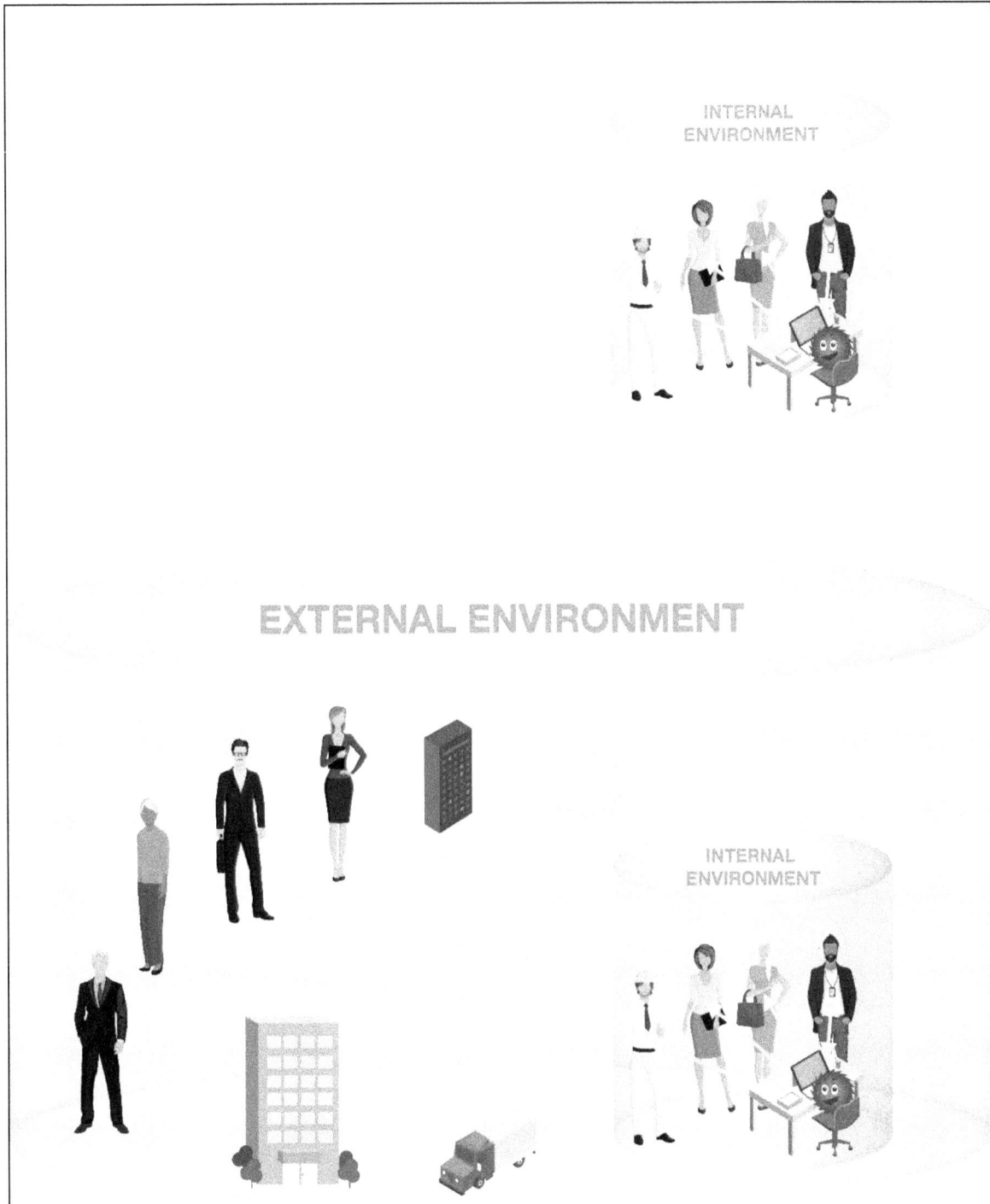

Flow

PROCESS FLOW

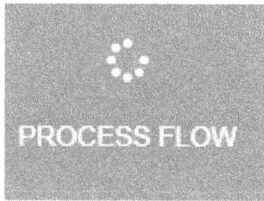

Step 2: Draw the 'flow' in the job. Every job has its own characteristic flow. There is always a point where the tasks start the job cycle and a point where they end it, only to start again. This cycle is the "Process Flow".

It's an advantage for an employee to diagram the typical job *flow* soon after starting the job. Most jobs have a sequential pattern of things to do. Other jobs have a basic flow but the incumbents may have to tackle some steps in 'interrupt mode' where they must attend to something immediately and then get back to the normal flow and rhythm of the job.

In a supermarket, most activities are performed in a logical sequence with obvious start and completion points. However, sometimes a cashier must react in 'interrupt mode' where a shopper may need attention for something that typically happens later in the process flow, like payment using separate credit cards. A Flow Chart can diagram the typical and alternative sequences of things to do in a job.

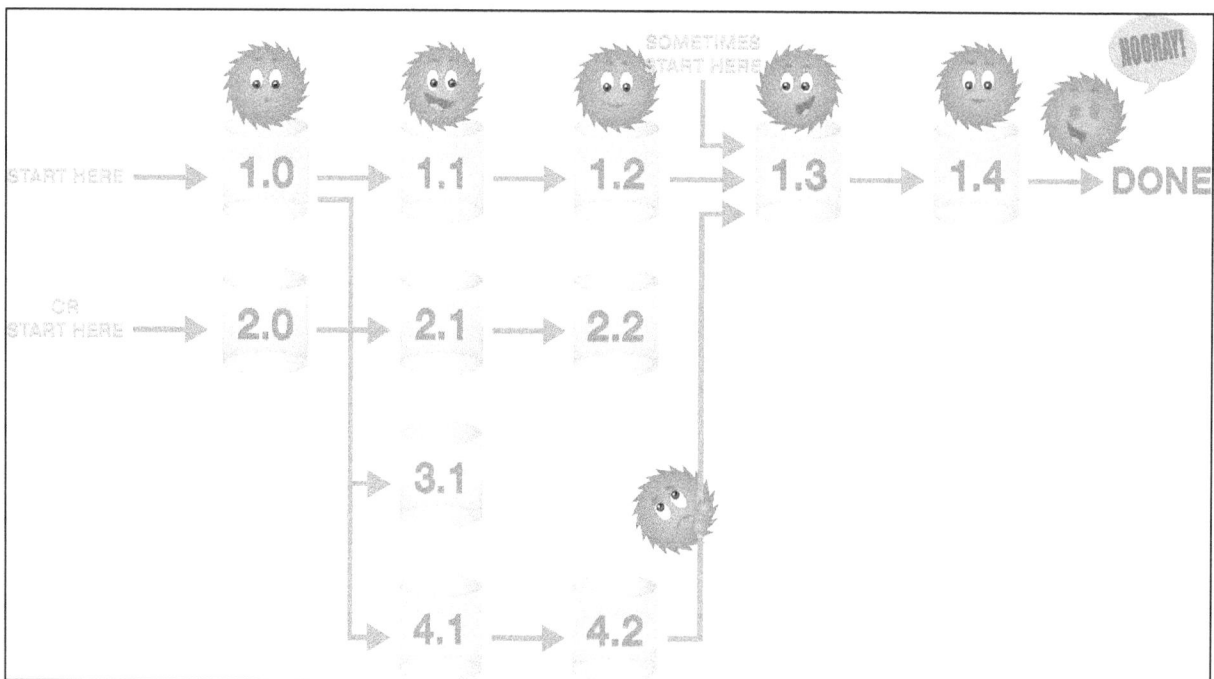

INs and OUTs

Step 3: For each process in the Flow Chart, compile an INs and OUTs diagram. Every job has processes that must be applied to certain inputs to produce specific outputs.

INs AND OUTs

Examine the occupation's Process Flow diagram from Step 2 with people experienced in the job. They will quickly reveal which 20% of the inputs and processes get performed 80% of the time.

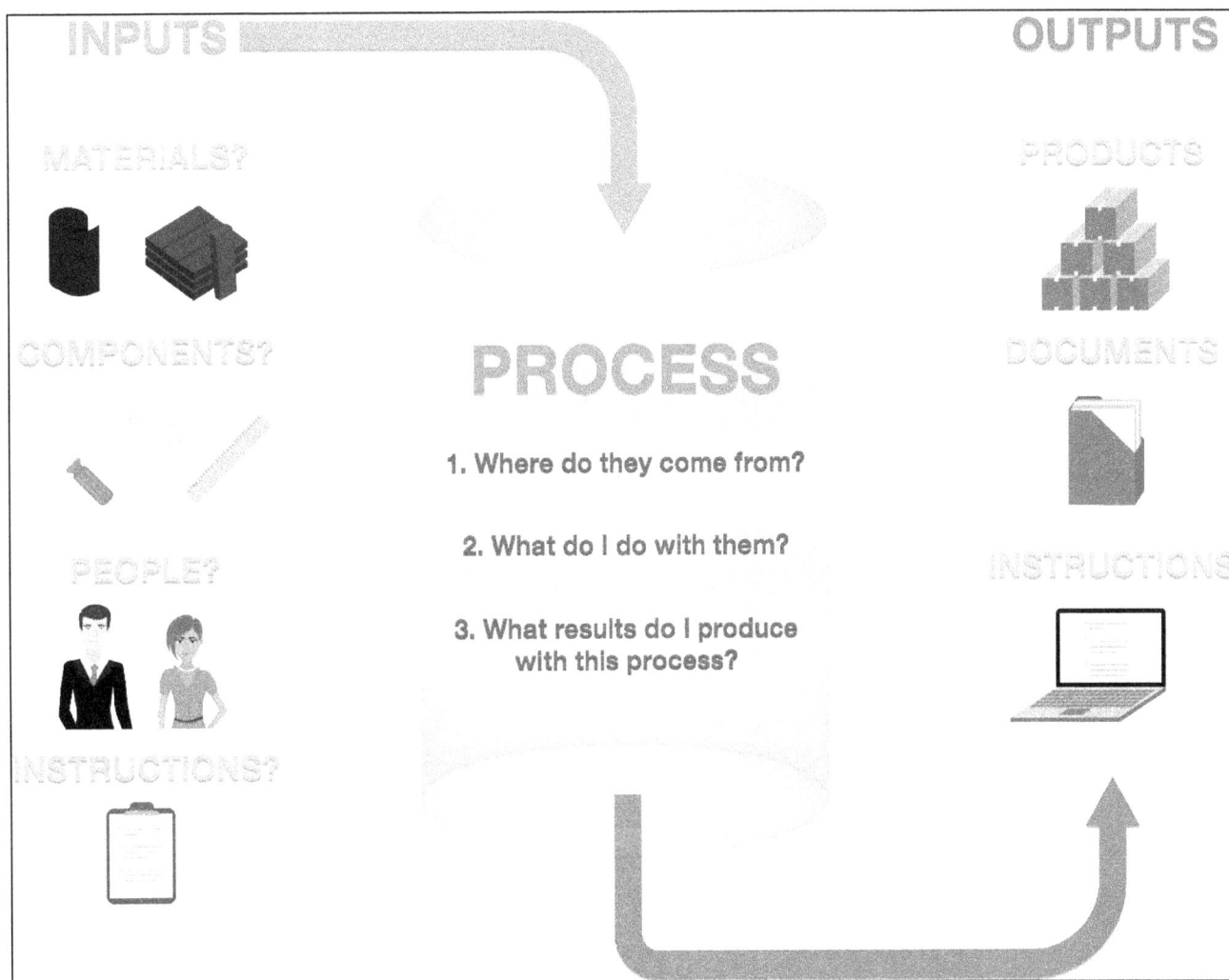

INPUTS

MATERIALS?

COMPONENTS?

PEOPLE?

INSTRUCTIONS?

PROCESS

1. Where do they come from?

2. What do I do with them?

3. What results do I produce with this process?

OUTPUTS

PRODUCTS

DOCUMENTS

INSTRUCTIONS

It will be worth taking a deeper look into at least those few processes and, at minimum, produce an INs and OUTs chart for each of them. Each process should be analyzed in the same way.

Every process in a job produces **outputs**. Outputs can be things like products, or completed tasks, completed entries in a software application, or entries on required paperwork. Outputs may be the result of services, for example, a clean, washed and well performing vehicle after maintenance at a vehicle dealership.

Outputs result from applying certain **process steps** to specific **inputs**. (Figure 4) In employees' jobs, it's an advantage for them to quickly establish which **specific process steps** must be applied to which materials, supplies, documents or people (**inputs**) in order to produce the required results (**outputs**).

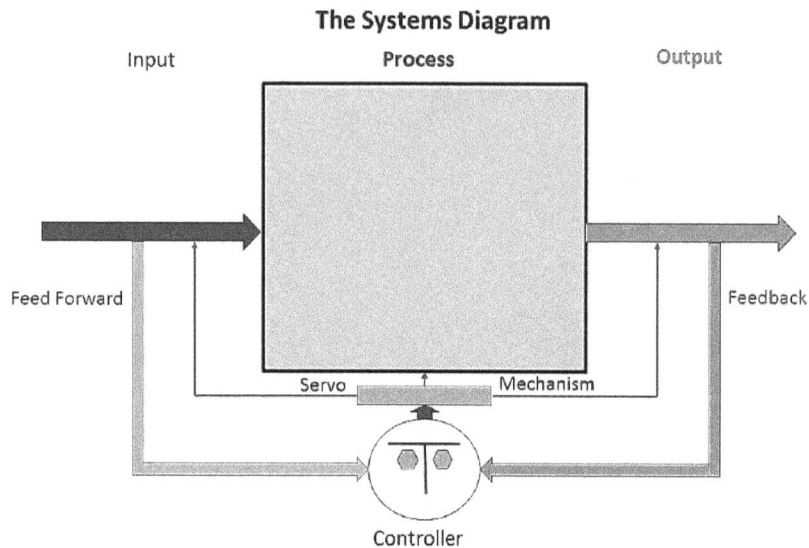

The Systems Diagram

Input   Process   Output

Feed Forward   Feedback

Servo   Mechanism

Controller

Figure 4 Diagram showing that a *Process* needs *Inputs* to produce *Outputs*

In a job, the employee is the 'Controller' ensuring that the process steps are applied correctly to the correct inputs to produce the required outputs. Each employee must know how to control **each** process in the job.

Every process should have feedback mechanisms that measure the inputs, process steps and outputs. Feedback mechanisms may be dials, dashboards, electronic or mechanical measuring devices or even just human body language that tells the employee exactly what's been done. The measurements they report will be 'Feedback' to the employee.

The company should also have some published standards and specifications for the materials, supplies, process steps and outputs. These are the employee's 'Feed Forward'. When the feedback matches the required feed forward, the process is under control. When the feedback does not match the feed forward, the employee will need to take corrective action to restore control and bring everything back to the required conditions and quality.

In practice, we find that looking at each process in an occupation from this perspective is the fastest way to understand all the elements in the job content. You can read as many manuals on the job as you like, but none will quickly provide this simple, **visual** perspective.

Frequency

Step 4: Analyze the frequency of tasks in the job. Every job has processes and tasks that occur with different frequencies. Some tasks must be performed much more often than others.

This is probably **the most important** job perspective for an employee to understand about their job. It's an advantage to know the tasks that are repeated more often than other tasks. Once an employee understands which tasks must be performed more often and which tasks occur less frequently, they will know the relative importance of the elements in their job.

An economist and statistician, Vilfredo Pareto[1], is famous for his 20/80 principle. Based on his principle, 20% of all the tasks in a job will be performed about 80% of the time.

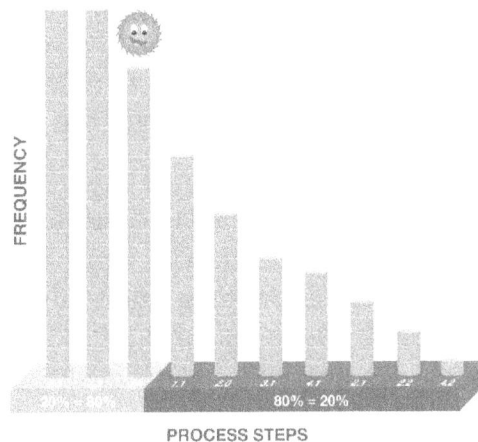

Figure 5 Identify the 20% to be performed 80% of the time.

As employees perfect their skills **first** in those 20% tasks, they will quickly achieve high productivity and best quality results in their job 80% of the time. (Figure 5) It also follows that 20% of the possible faults in a job occur 80% of the time. If the employee learns what these are, early in the job, the incumbent will be able to anticipate them and avoid problems through quick recognition of symptoms for developing faults.

---

[1] **Vilfredo Federico Damaso Pareto** (born *Wilfried Fritz Pareto*; Italian:5 July 1848 – 19 August 1923) was an Italian engineer, sociologist, economist, political scientist, and philosopher. He made several important contributions to economics, particularly in the study of income distribution, and in the analysis of individuals' choices. He was also responsible for popularizing the use of the term "elite" in social analysis. He introduced the concept of Pareto efficiency and helped develop the field of microeconomics. He was also the first to discover that income follows a Pareto distribution. (Wikipedia)

Of course, in an occupation it's not easy to analyze these 20/80 incidences scientifically. In some jobs, companies have records that permit the tracking of fault frequencies. In most cases, employees and mentors need to rely on the opinions of those with years of experience on the job. In this book, we'll provide suggested things to do and questions to ask to capture both the list of processes and tasks; and the list of faults, their symptoms, their probable causes and the required corrective actions. The 7 Steps software application allows the capturing of all of these elements.

Checklists

Step 5: Generate checklists. Every job needs one or more checklists to ensure that the correct steps and actions will be performed in the right sequence, to the required quality, at the required cost and within all safety requirements.

No one understands the need for checklists more than a pilot or an astronaut. In flying or space travel, there is always more than one person who deals with the checklists. Obviously, in flying, there is the concern for the safety of passengers that drives the strict attention to correct setup of systems, processes and monitoring devices.

Once employees understand the processes, inputs and outputs in a job, they're ready to use detailed *checklists* especially as they begin to perform the job. It may not be necessary to have a checklist for every one of the processing steps in the job, but it's highly advisable to create checklists at least for the 20% of processes that are performed 80% of the time. If the steps in some of the **low frequency** job processes are complex, or critical to safety, quality or cost, it is advisable to develop checklists for some of them as well. The 7 Steps software application generates checklists automatically once you have completed capturing the INs and OUTs for each process step.

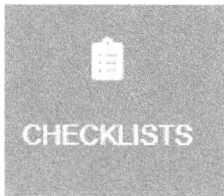

We also provide an app in the Apple Store (for iPhones and iPads) and Google Play (Android devices) for viewing checklists on-demand as the employee may need them on the job. The 7 Steps app for checklists and faults can be downloaded from the Apple Store and Google Play.

Faults

Step 6: Compile a list of the faults that may occur in the job. In every job, things go wrong. Some things go wrong more often than others.

The Pareto 20/80 principle applies to faults on the job. It's important to analyze fault frequencies in jobs where historical statistics are available. Otherwise, an employee needs to be proactive and ask people with years of experience on the job about the typical fault conditions that might occur.

When an occupation Researcher schedules time to talk to people with experience on a job and anyone responsible for oversight and quality control for the job, they soon discover they can compile a list of job faults. They can then rank the faults by classifying them as an "A" (High Frequency Fault), "B" (Medium Frequency Fault) and "C" (Low Frequency Fault). This is called the "A-B-C" Analysis.

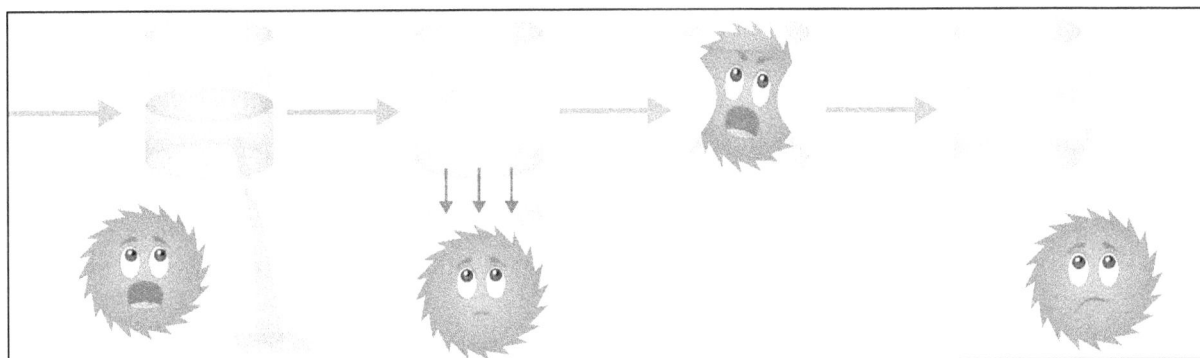

Each fault has elements with which the employee needs to become familiar:

Symptoms: Like human illnesses, each fault has characteristic symptoms. The earlier the employee detects a fault condition developing, the better. Early detection allows the employee to get things back to normal and head off avoidable, costly damage. If employees learn to recognize and identify **symptoms,** they can stop serious fault conditions developing.

Probable Causes: Typically, there is more than one reason why a specific fault condition develops. The occupation Researcher should talk to people with more experience in the job and anyone responsible for oversight and quality control for the job. They'll quickly learn that there can be more than one cause of the fault.   Employees need to ensure that they're addressing the **correct cause** before applying any adjustments. If they apply the wrong corrective action - because they've identified the fault incorrectly, they may end up with even more damage.

Corrective Action: Each 'Cause' requires the appropriate Corrective Action.

Once employees have their list of faults ranked in the A-B-C sequence, they can quickly add the list of symptoms, probable causes and then, for each **probable cause**, add the required corrective action.

Know that things will go wrong in a job. If employees equip themselves to recognize the symptoms for the 20% of faults that happen 80% of the time, they'll be on top of the job out of the starting blocks. Hopefully, a mentor can help the employee find someone who can explain the **critical** low frequency faults that occur. Employees need to know how to apply fast corrective responses to those symptoms as well or know when to get help from an experienced employee. With the help of an experienced colleague who can simulate or re-create such a fault, employees can learn how to react. However, employees need to experience a high enough frequency of those low frequency faults before they will have the 'experience' to apply the correct responses themselves.

Patrolling

PATROL

Step 7: Develop a Patrol Pattern and Inspection Sequence. Success depends on correct performance in many locations in the job and at many process points.

Once employees know the 20% of **tasks** that must be performed 80% of the time and also know the 20% of the **faults** that occur 80% of the time, they soon realize that they can prevent serious problems by patrolling their job territories. It makes sense that they should move around the different people and points of processing in their job to check that things are correct. While doing this patrol, employees should look for symptoms of developing faults. When they find a fault developing, they immediately address it appropriately to restore things to controlled conditions. Top performers stay on top of things by using this technique.

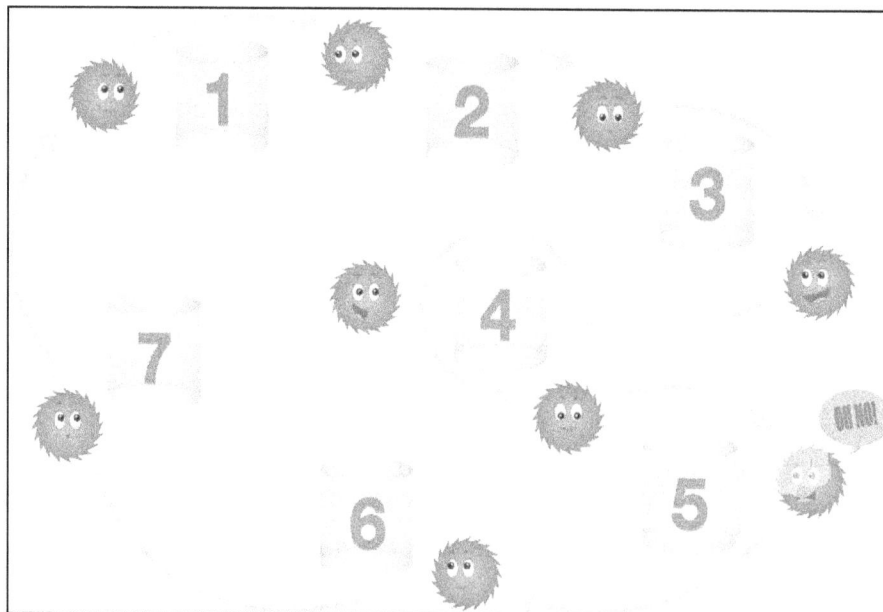

1	Environment	Define the job's environments. Every job operates within definable environments. You can describe these as *internal* and *external* environments.	ENVIRONMENT
2	Process Flow	Draw the 'flow' in the job. Every job has its own characteristic flow. There is always a point where the tasks start the job cycle and a point where they end it, only to start again. This cycle is the "Process Flow".	PROCESS FLOW
3	INs and OUTs	For each process in the Flow Chart, compile an INs and OUTs diagram. Every job has processes that must be applied to certain inputs to produce specific outputs.	INs AND OUTs
4	Frequency	Analyze the frequency of tasks in the job. Every job has processes and tasks that occur with different frequencies. Some tasks must be performed much more often than others.	FREQUENCY
5	Checklists	Generate checklists for critical processes. Every job needs one or more checklists to ensure that the correct steps and actions will be performed in the right sequence, to the required quality, at the required cost and within all safety requirements.	CHECKLISTS
6	Faults	Compile a list of the faults that may occur in the job. In every job, things go wrong. Some things go wrong more often than others.	FAULTS
7	Patrolling	Develop a Patrol Pattern and Inspection Sequence. Success depends on correct performance in many locations in the job and at many process points.	PATROL

Figure 6 Summary of the 7 Steps recommended and explained in this book.

Summary of the 7 Steps

So, there you have it. These are the 7 Steps for quickly understanding an occupation and becoming successful in record time. (Figure 6)

In the chapters that follow, we provide a clear explanation of each step. The 7 Steps software application facilitates fast capture of the content for each of the seven steps. For anyone who does not have a computer, blank copies of the 7 Step forms for manual processing are provided on the www.7stepslms.com website for mentors and employees to copy and use.

We suggest the best questions to ask as an assigned 'occupation Researcher'. This will help the Occupation Researcher to get as much information as needed to be successful capturing all the required content for developing a learning experience.

There are no hard and fast rules for how each technique applies. It's not suggested that mentors require employees to wait until they've completed the analyses before starting the job. Indeed, analyses should start as soon as scheduled and should then be updated and amended as more information about the job is assembled. Although we recommend that job Researchers try to follow the steps in sequence, this may not always be possible. Typically, experienced employees start telling you things in **their** sequence. Some get confused when you try to get them to complete one-step at a time.

Mentors should encourage job Researchers to make notes as they capture information and then key it into the 7 Steps software application.

| 7. PATROLLING |
| 6. FAULTS |
| 5. CHECKLISTS |
| 4. FREQUENCY |
| 3. INs and OUTs |
| 2. FLOW |
| 1. ENVIRONMENT |

Figure 7 The 7 Steps Layers

CHAPTER 3   WHAT'S THE JOB ENVIRONMENT

Step 1: Define the job's environments. Every job operates within definable environments. You can describe these as internal and external environments.

Internal Environment

When trying to understand the job, the Occupation Researcher can examine the Internal Environment from two points of view:

Firstly: The immediate workspace – the **space** and **things** they'll **use** in the job

Secondly: The **things and people** with whom they'll **interact** within that immediate space.

Firstly, the employee needs to identify the **space** in which they'll **perform** the job and the **things** they'll need in **that space** to perform each of the tasks. Some jobs occur at a desk or counter. Some occur in 'walkable space' like a restaurant, a workshop or retail store. Some jobs occur over a distance like travelling sales jobs, or Internet-based activities from home.

When occupation Researchers diagram the internal environment for a position, they'll start with opinions from those who are mentoring them. Each Researcher must be alert to the fact that the results of their exploration may not be the best layout for the job. They can begin with diagramming or photographing the mentor's suggestions, but they may jointly discover ways to improve the layout of the space to make it more logical and productive for workers.

It's recommended that Researchers photograph that space and all the things an employee will **use** in that space. They can show the percentage interaction with the elements in the space using the 7 Steps application Internal Environment capture page. Researchers can also make extensive use of their smartphone camera to help here. Use it to capture images of the workspace for people in the job. Researchers should take closer shots of the things employees will be using such as equipment, facilities, documents, and appliances (including their computer, printer, work tops, tools, rubber stamps, lockable drawers, etc.) and then capture the images in the 7 Steps application.

Example 1: Restaurant Server's – Internal Environment

Let's start with a job that should be familiar to all of us, a Server waiting tables in a restaurant.

(Source: Google Images)

Typically, Servers are assigned a certain number of tables for which they'll be responsible. A job entrant certainly needs to understand the location and boundaries of the assigned territory. Figure 8 shows the layout of the restaurant with that all-important layout of tables for the 'new' Server (Figure 93). We see the location of the new Server's territory in relation to the territories for the experienced Servers.

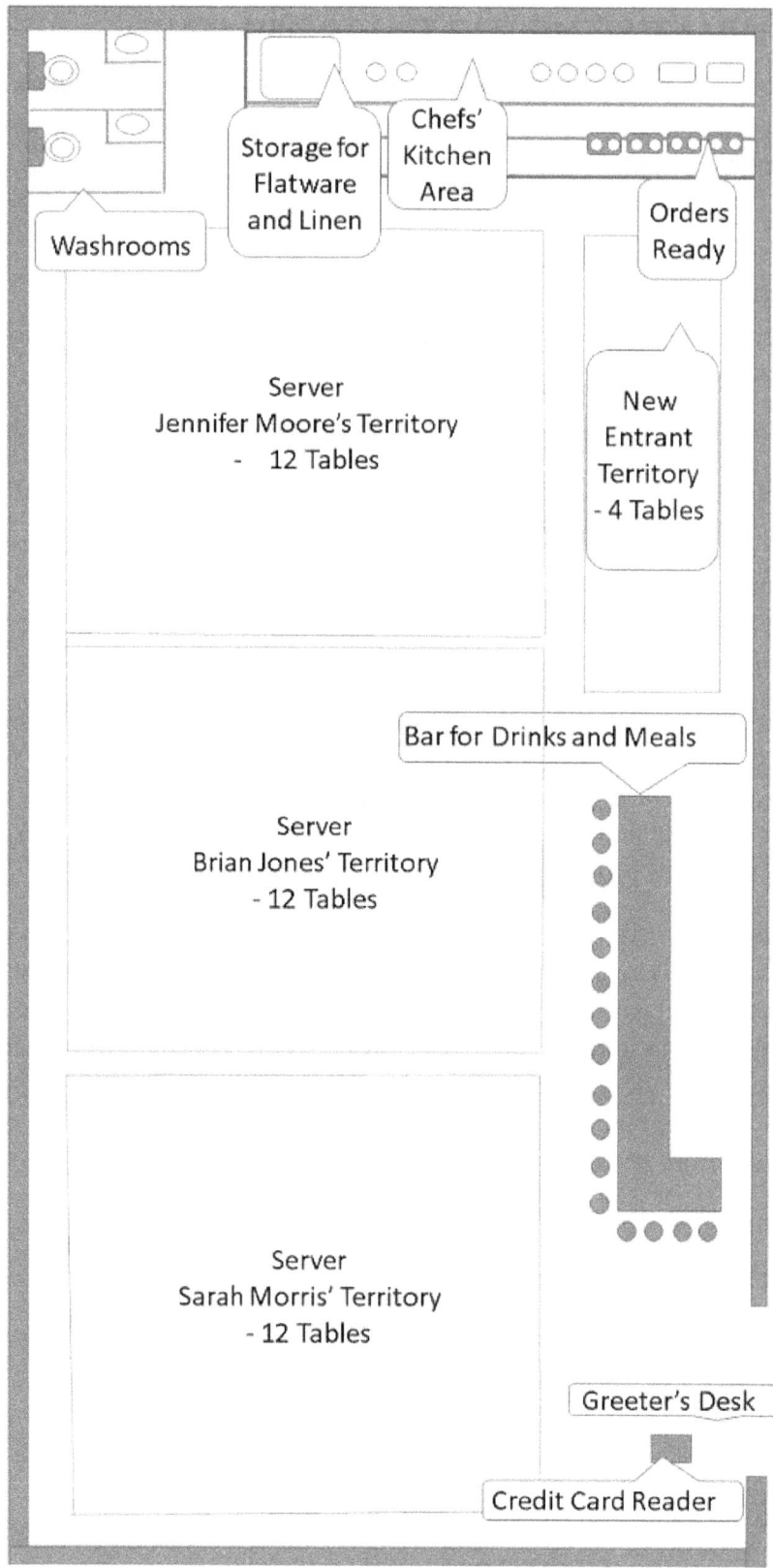

Figure 8 Simple Internal Environment for a Restaurant Server

We also see the location of the Chef's kitchen and the placement of orders 'ready-for-delivery'. We see the location of the bar for preparing drinks. We note that the credit card reader is located at the Greeter's desk. This is a simple Internal Environment.

In the case of a Restaurant Server, it would also be appropriate to make a sketch or take photographs from different angles of the required table layout showing the correct positioning of flatware, napkins, and glasses. (Figure 9)

Restaurant Server's Internal Environment – Organization of Elements

Figure 9 The required table layout
(Source: Google Images)

The Internal Environment should show the best and most productive layout for the job. When things are in the right place, the job occupant can perform the job with the least amount of wasted effort. This internal environment photograph shows the required layout for cutlery, plates, glasses and a fragrant candle. It shows the required positioning for the chairs before customers arrive to be seated. Once reviewed and approved by the Researcher's mentor, the diagrams and photos should be uploaded into the 7 Steps section for environment images and pictures.

Internal Environment

The first part of Step 1 Environments helps the employee understand the spatial and people relationships in the job. It's important first to understand the Internal Environment before Researchers try to understand the relevance of any interaction with people **outside** their job's immediate workspace.

For Researchers who haven't performed the job to document the job's Internal Environment, they need to work with a manager or a mentor who has performed in the job recently. When setting out to ask the questions about the Internal Environment, the Researcher could print the "Things to Do" and "Questions to Ask" from the 7 Step application and make notes on the back. They could also use a copy of the 7 Steps Internal Environment Worksheet. The worksheet has example questions printed on the back of the sheet to help the employee when meeting with the mentor.

Once employees understand the best layout for their job, they should move to an understanding of the immediate people relationships they'll depend on in the job. The 7 Steps application helps present the job in a circle in the center with arrowed spokes radiating outwards. There should be one spoke for each of the things and people with whom they'll interact. The width of each spoke should indicate the relative amount of time they'll interact with each. (Figure 10)

Example 2: Supermarket Cashier's Internal Environment

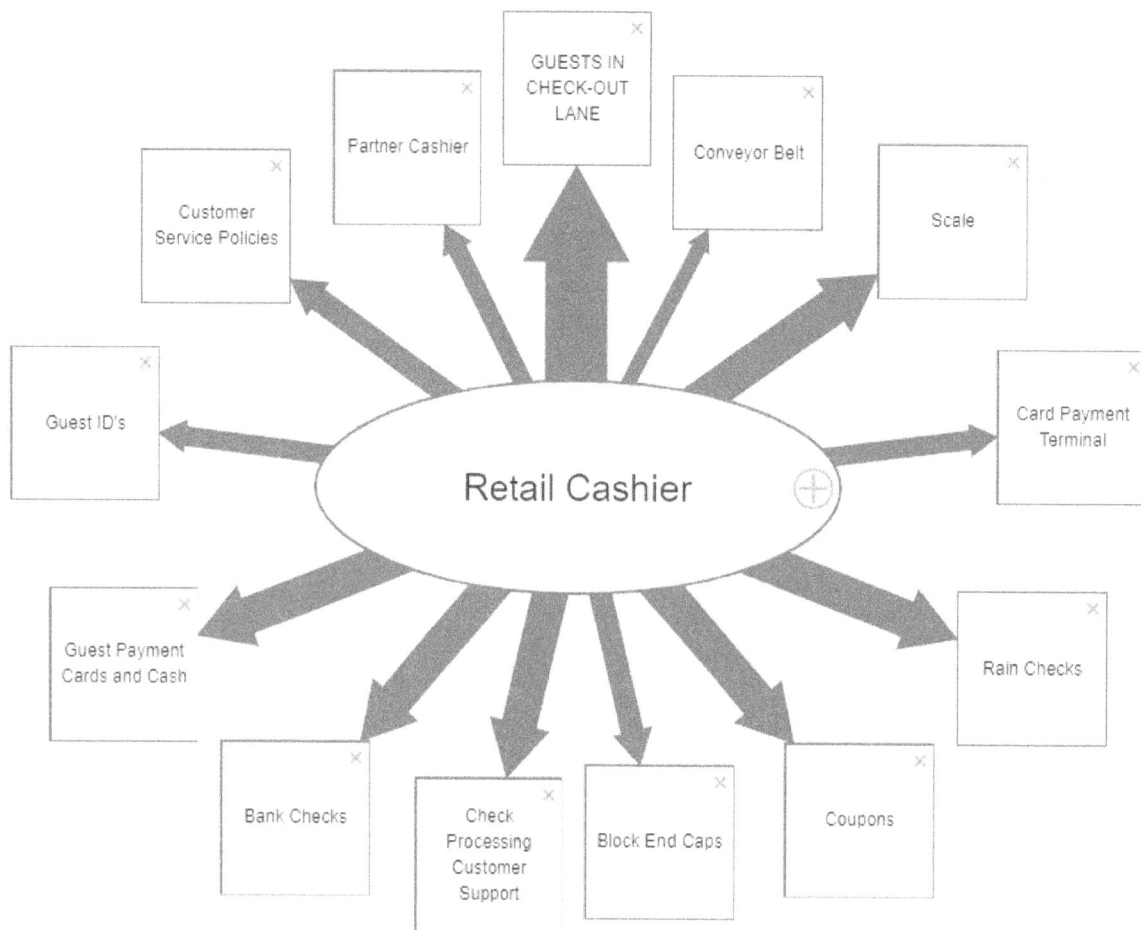

Figure 10 Example Supermarket Cashier's Internal Environment

Things to Do and Questions to Ask to Determine the Job's Internal Environment

Here are some example 'Things to Do' and questions to prompt discussion with a selected mentor. Researchers will find that once they get started in discussions, things begin to flow smoothly. (Remember the value of a pencil and eraser. Often mentors make changes once they see your diagrams and notes emerging.)

Things to Do

- Get a copy of the current organization chart covering the job area.

- Get a copy of the current company phone list and highlight the names of the people with whom the employee will interact most frequently.

- Diagram the first draft of the layout of the workspace.

- Take photographs of the workspace. Employees should be careful to take the photographs as the worker's eyes see things when working. Keep remembering to "See it as the EYE sees it."

- Label the diagrams and photographs.

- Make time to review the information with your mentors.

Questions to Ask

- When last did you work in this job? (Obviously, employees need to be getting mentoring from someone who has recent experience in that job.)

- Will you help me understand some of the elements of the job?

- Can you help me diagram the layout of the place of work and point out the things the worker will be using in the job, for example, equipment, tools, facilities, electronics, software, and security systems, etc.?

- Can you point out the best angles to photograph the elements in this space so that I can see what things are used and where they must be kept?

- Can you point out where materials, parts and documents come from to be processed in this environment?

- Where exactly do the materials, parts and documents enter the process?

- How do they get to where it must go?

- Where does the completed output go?

- How does the completed output get there?

- What signage is important to this position?

- What regulations are important to this position?

Figure 11 Examples of Safety Signs

In-Company Mentors need to ensure that employees participating in these 7 Step projects understand and identify the signage related to the job. If these are available in print, Researchers should get copies, photograph them and upload them into the developing 7 Steps Internal Environment. There will be safety signage (Figure 11) and probably posters related to employment regulations. It's also important to understand where materials, supplies and paperwork come from and where they go.

Most jobs come under OSHA Safety Regulations. Secure a digital file of the regulations or scan them and upload them into the 7 Steps Internal environment. In a Union environment, there'll be booklets, documents and signage that influence Union employees' approaches to their jobs.

If employees will work with Union members, they must know the regulations that affect them. Secure a digital file of the regulations or scan them and upload them into the 7 Steps Masterfile.

External Environment

The External Environment study relates to how the employee's job will interact with organizations and people **outside** the space in which they operate. With the External Environment diagram, Figure 12, the job name will appear in a center hub from which spokes radiate. The Researcher's diagram should reveal the required relationships with people, departments and companies **outside** the job's **internal** workspace. These are typically customers, agents, resellers, distributors, suppliers, payment processors, banks, insurers, legal advisors, auditors, quality control personnel, and area-, region- or corporate-management with whom the job entrant may be required to interact on occasions. The interaction may also be with external software applications, websites or social media sites used in the job. Once again, we suggest that the size of the 'interactions arrow' should reflect the extent of the probable interaction.

Example 3: Supermarket Cashier's External Environment

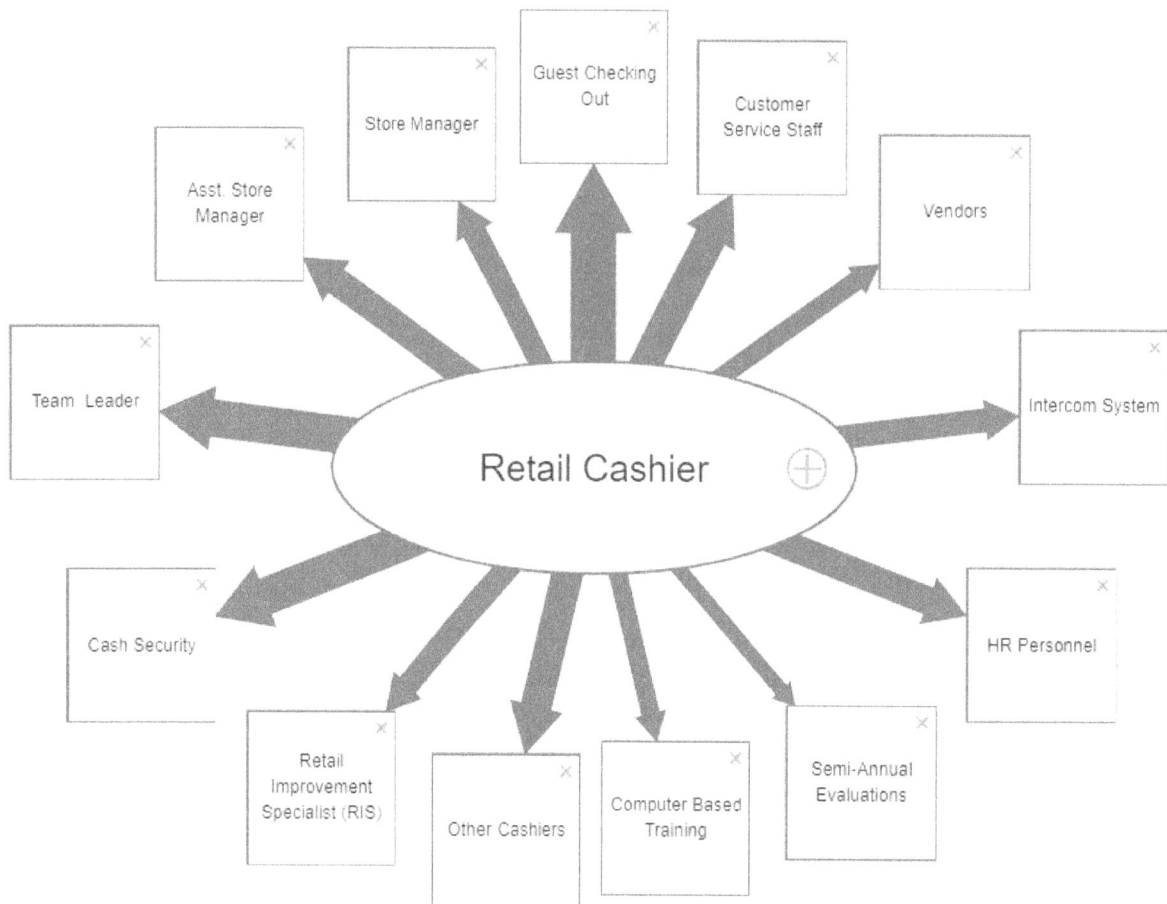

Figure 12 Example of the Supermarket Cashier's External Environment

Most of the Supermarket Cashier's interaction is related to Guest Check outs. Since they are not employees, guests are in the External Environment. Note that the arrows show there is more interaction with the Assistant Manager than the Store Manager and even more with the Team Leader.

Things to Do and Questions to Ask to Determine the Job's External Environment

Things to Do
- Schedule Time with the Supervisor or Manager and the selected mentors to capture their information about the interaction patterns in the job.

Questions to Ask
- What are all the 'outside' occupations and organizations that influence this job?

- What's the name of each organization or person with whom the employee must interact? What is their title?

- Why do they need the results from what this job does?

- Which environment elements will the employee interact with more often than others?

- Who supplies things to the employee in this job?

- Why do I need the things they provide?

Why Capture and Diagram the Environments?

Now that you've seen some examples of the internal environment layout and internal interactive diagrams together with the external interactive environment charts, you should realize that it doesn't take long to capture and build these views of the job. Once the employee understands the 'space' they'll be working in, as defined by the internal and external environments, they'll quickly capture information about the elements, content and people in the job.

Perhaps even more important is that they'll be going outward bound to spend time with people in the company who might influence their progress in the organization. Many employees feel important when asked to 'mentor' other employees.

CHAPTER 4 WHAT'S THE FLOW IN THE JOB?

Step 2: Draw the 'flow' in the job. Every job has its own characteristic flow. There is always a point where the tasks start and a point where they end the job cycle, only to start again. This is the "Process Flow".

It's an advantage to diagram the typical job flow. All jobs have a **sequence** of processes to be performed. Some processes take input from other jobs along the way. Outputs may go to other occupations at the end of the employee's job cycle, or a process along the way might provide outputs to other jobs.

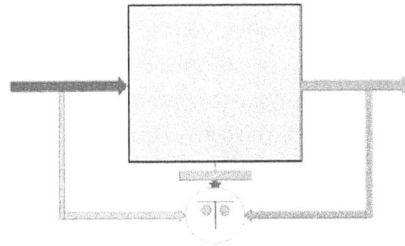

Figure 13 Icon favored when building a Process Flow Diagram

We like to use a small version of the 'INs and OUTs' icon when drawing a Process Flow. (The meaning of each of the components in this icon will be explained in more detail in the next chapter.) The resulting sequence of boxes will remind us that every job consists of **processes** required in the job. The INs and OUTs box shows that in each **process**, tasks must be applied to specific **inputs** in order to deliver the **outputs** required at that point of processing. The INs and OUTs box with its arrows also reminds us that every process needs to be monitored at each point to ensure you've got things in control and are delivering the correct outcomes.

Process Flow for a Supermarket Cashier

When we examine the example Process flow for a Supermarket Cashier, Figure 14, we see the typical steps in a normal shift:

• The Time Clocking procedure, and
• A review of the shift schedule and assigned duties for the shift
The shift commences with a group of activities in parallel
• A hand-over from the previous cashier on shift
o Reconciling the cash
o Check and clean the workstation
• Log-in to the guest check out systems
• Open the station for guest processing
Most of the shift then consists of:

• Check out guests
• Scan or weigh purchased items
• Process payments

When another cashier takes over, the cashier must Poll the till, counting and reconciling all the cash. At the end of a shift or at a Cashier Hand-over, the Cashier will perform the hand over and securely deposit any surplus cash. We see that there is a sequence to performing the tasks in the job. However, some tasks can be done in parallel or some may occur in 'interrupt mode'. This is an X-ray view of the job from a different point of view than the Environmental Analyses. (Figure 14)

Process Flow is the sequence of tasks in the job

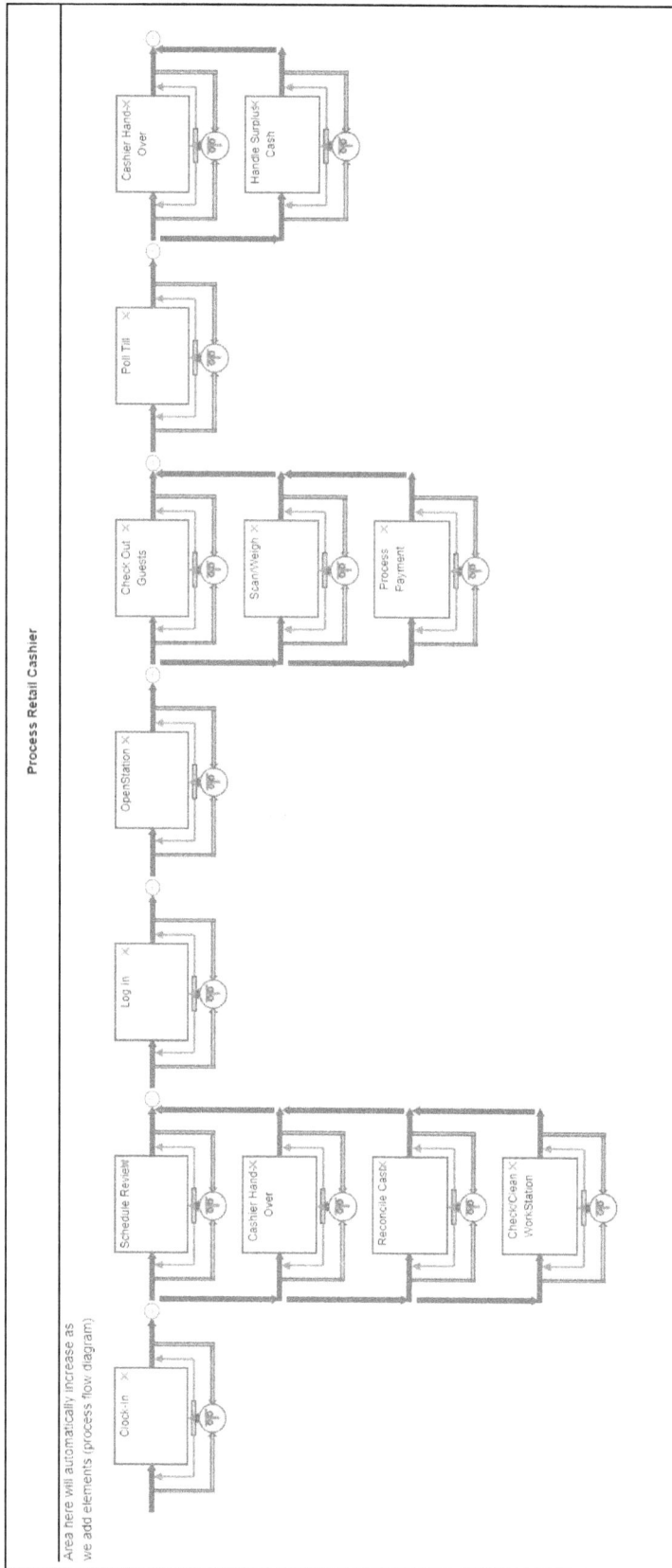

Figure 14 Example of a Process Flow Diagram in the 7 Steps Masterfile

The benefit of seeing the 'flow' in a job is to avoid confusion (Figure 14). Often, people teaching an employee to do a job, start teaching a process step that they know well. It's not until later that the employee gets to understand where **that process** fits in the general scheme of things. Until then, the employee may be confused as to which process must be applied before others. This can lead to considerable confusion and frustration in the early stages of doing the job on their own.

Be warned, try to protect a participating employee from being assigned a job mentor who is haphazard and doesn't address the processes in the job in the most logical way. As a result, tasks may be unnecessarily repeated. The first diagram of the process flow may not be the best or optimum flow for the job. Encourage Researchers to test their Process Flow diagram with other mentors and get their suggestions on the most logical flow.

This Process Flow style of analysis applies to any job, whether it's serving in a fast food store, driving trucks or buses, or doing really sophisticated jobs like engineering design. It applies to teaching and lecturing. It applies to nursing and medical practice. In fact, we believe there is no job that can't be diagrammed in this way to the benefit of job entrants.

Things to Do and Questions to Ask to Determine the Job's Process Flow

Things to Do
- Request help to build a list of the main steps in the cycle of the job.

- Then get help in sequencing them into the most logical order.

- Determine which must be performed before the other. Remember that some things may happen daily while others may happen weekly, monthly, quarterly or annually. At first, you just want to find out **what** flows to **what**.

Questions to Ask
- Can you help me diagram a chart that shows the steps or processes in the job using little boxes and arrows? I need to show:
    - **What** comes from **where**
    - The **name** of each process step, and
    - **Where** the output from that process goes next.
- Can you give me an idea of the steps or processes in a typical job cycle?
    - Where does the work begin?
    - Where does it go to from there?
    - Where does it end and then start all over again?

- What processes can be performed in 'parallel' to any main process step?

- Where does the output from an earlier process step become the input to one of the parallel steps?

- Is there anywhere where an input comes from another department or person and enters the job at a process point further down the line of flow? Can we identify where it comes from?

- Where does the output from each process step go next?

Once the employee has captured their interpretation of the internal and external environments and have an understanding of the process flow in the job, it's time to start probing deeper into the job content. Even if the employees have performed this kind of job before, they'll need to understand what's unique about the inputs, processes and outputs required in that position. A new organization may process things the employee has done before in a different way – for example, using different paperwork and software.

On completion of the Process Flow analysis, the Researcher moves to creating an INs and OUTs chart for each of the steps in the Process Flow.

CHAPTER 5   INS AND OUTS

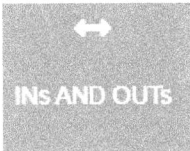

INs AND OUTs

Step 3: For each process in the Flow Chart, compile an INs and OUTs diagram. Every job has processes that must be applied to certain inputs to produce specific outputs.

The Job Description

We recommend Researchers begin diagramming 'INs and OUTs' at the highest-level first, that is, a summary of the total job. If the Researcher has completed the Environment Analyses and Process Flow chart, they'll move to the 'INs and OUTs' option in the 7 Steps menu. This will provide an INs and OUTs capture tool. 7 Steps generates a blank INs & OUTs capture page for the defined occupation and then for each of the steps in the Process Flow chart. We recommend that one begins with the high-level summary of the job (literally a one-page Job Description). This will result in a Job Description looking like this, for example, for a Retail Cashier in a supermarket on one page. (See Figure 15.)

This may look complex at first, but it's actually the simplest expression of what the job is all about. Read the typical Job Description provided by an organization. It has lines and lines of text with no visual representation of what the job activities look like and how they fit in relation to each other. Then read the diagram below: Outputs first, then the list of Inputs, and then the list of Processes.

Project Participants can then develop an INs and OUTs chart for each of the listed processes, for example, in Figure 15, that's an example of sixteen **processes** listed for the job of a supermarket cashier.

The high-level Job Summary diagram will have different content for different jobs. In this example, we have referred only to supermarket cashiers. Obviously, the processes, inputs and outputs will be different for different jobs.

As they capture the INs and OUTs for each process, Researchers should identify the frequency with which each element occurs in the job. This can be done simply by assigning an "A" (High Frequency), "B" (Medium Frequency) or "C" (Low Frequency) next to each line item as the Researcher captures the output-, input-, and process-items.

As Researchers complete their INs and OUTs diagrams, they should show them to their content specialist, job manager and assigned mentor. A 'Best Practice' is to review their Environment studies, their Process Flow chart and their INs and OUTs diagrams together with as many advisors that influence successful performance in the job.

The Job Description on ONE page

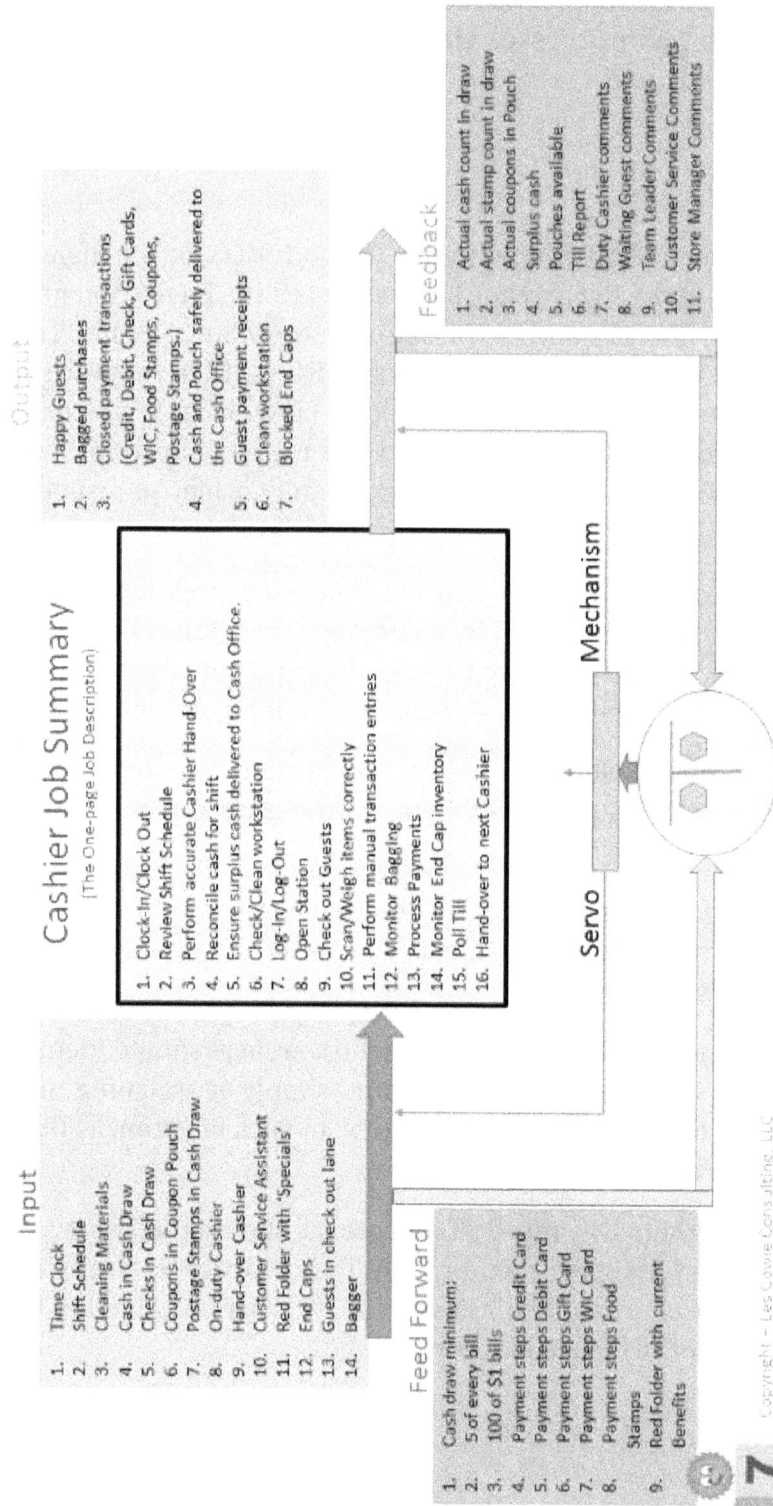

Input

1. Time Clock
2. Shift Schedule
3. Cleaning Materials
4. Cash in Cash Draw
5. Checks In Cash Draw
6. Coupons in Coupon Pouch
7. Postage Stamps in Cash Draw
8. On-duty Cashier
9. Hand-over Cashier
10. Customer Service Assistant
11. Red Folder with 'Specials'
12. End Caps
13. Guests in check out lane
14. Bagger

Feed Forward

1. Cash draw minimum:
2. 5 of every bill
3. 100 of $1 bills
4. Payment steps Credit Card
5. Payment steps Debit Card
6. Payment steps Gift Card
7. Payment steps WIC Card
8. Payment steps Food
9. Stamps
   Red Folder with current
   Benefits

Cashier Job Summary
(The One-page Job Description)

1. Clock-In/Clock Out
2. Review Shift Schedule
3. Perform accurate Cashier Hand-Over
4. Reconcile cash for shift
5. Ensure surplus cash delivered to Cash Office.
6. Check/Clean workstation
7. Log-In/Log-Out
8. Open Station
9. Check out Guests
10. Scan/Weigh items correctly
11. Perform manual transaction entries
12. Monitor Bagging
13. Process Payments
14. Monitor End Cap inventory
15. Poll Till
16. Hand-over to next Cashier

Output

1. Happy Guests
2. Bagged purchases
3. Closed payment transactions (Credit, Debit, Check, Gift Cards, WIC, Food Stamps, Coupons, Postage Stamps.)
4. Cash and Pouch safely delivered to the Cash Office
5. Guest payment receipts
6. Clean workstation
7. Blocked End Caps

Feedback

1. Actual cash count in draw
2. Actual stamp count in draw
3. Actual coupons in Pouch
4. Surplus cash
5. Pouches available
6. Till Report
7. Duty Cashier comments
8. Waiting Guest comments
9. Team Leader Comments
10. Customer Service Comments
11. Store Manager Comments

Servo

Mechanism

Copyright – Les Cowie Consulting, LLC

Figure 15 Example of an INs and OUTs analysis for a Supermarket Cashier

Feed Forward and Feedback

Many people have learned the steps required to do a job. Unfortunately, instructors often don't teach the targets or **standards** to be reached in the job, so employees often don't know when they are performing up to standard. Even professional learning experience developers make this mistake. Often, job entrants are not taught the 'Feedback' systems that apply in the job. Even worse, they're often not taught the expectations or standards for the job ('Feeds Forward').

Think of an aircraft pilot. It's one thing for a pilot to know how to take-off, fly and land an aircraft but where do the passengers find themselves when the pilot discovers that he has not arrived at the correct destination airport. What if he suddenly finds that the plane is running out of fuel? What if he suddenly learns that the landing gear is stuck when approaching the runway?

Pilots have a set of screens, gauges, lights and warning sounds that reassure them that everything is in control. A gauge may have an indicator that marks what a specific flight condition **should be**. Industrial engineers call this a "standard". Most engineers call it a "Feed Forward" because the device or flight manual feeds the required standard to the pilot in advance of performing an action. The gauges or devices display the 'actual' condition. Engineers call this "Feedback".

To bring it closer to home, think of the navigation system you have on your smartphone or on the dashboard of your vehicle. When you set the destination, the navigation software illustrates the route you must take. This is supported by a calm voice that warns you of a pending change in direction. It alerts you in advance of you having to make the change. This is "Feed Forward". The navigation display then shows you where you actually are at any moment in time. This is "Feedback".

When the Feedback matches or equals the Feed Forward, everything is in control. So, when you're where you should be, everything is in control. However, a very important part of control is **knowing** the instant that Feedback doesn't match the Feed Forward because then things are moving out of control. A classic example of this is when you're driving, and you miss the recommended turn. That calm voice, sometimes irritatingly, keeps telling you: "Make a legal U-turn!"

Engineers design devices and systems that can make appropriate corrections automatically when a process starts going out of control. They typically call such an automatic corrective device or system a "Servomechanism". The servomechanism needs to determine the exact amount of corrective action needed to bring things back in control. In the case of making a U-turn, to get back on track and proceed correctly to the destination, a human performs as the 'servo-mechanism'. The human makes the correct turn at the right time as indicated by the navigation system.

Some jobs have automated systems built into the processes, for example, in robots used for vehicle assembly. Fortunately, most jobs require a human employee to keep things in control. To do this, the employee on the job must know the specifications and standards required in the job and what Feedback systems there are that signal when things are out of control and require the human to intervene and act as a servomechanism.

Most companies publish company policies. All companies have to display or make available, government regulations concerning safety and health as they relate to the job and its environment. Even if a job doesn't have **published** specifications, there are expectations set by others who provide input or use the output from the job. Sometimes employees have to learn these expectations as they proceed in the job. The sooner employees can capture and document the Feeds Forward and the Feeds Back, the sooner they'll become known for their accuracy and excellence.

The model we use is one that software developers have been using for years in the creation of complex software applications. It's called: "The Systems Diagram". (See Figure 16.)

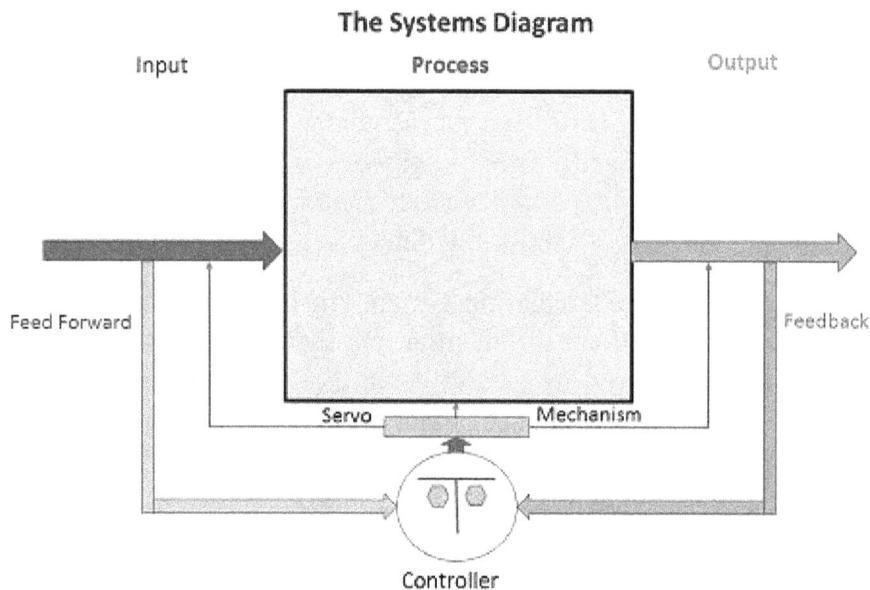

Figure 16 Illustration of the Engineering Systems Diagram.

Here's what the total 'Systems Diagram' (Job Description) will look like for a Restaurant Server:

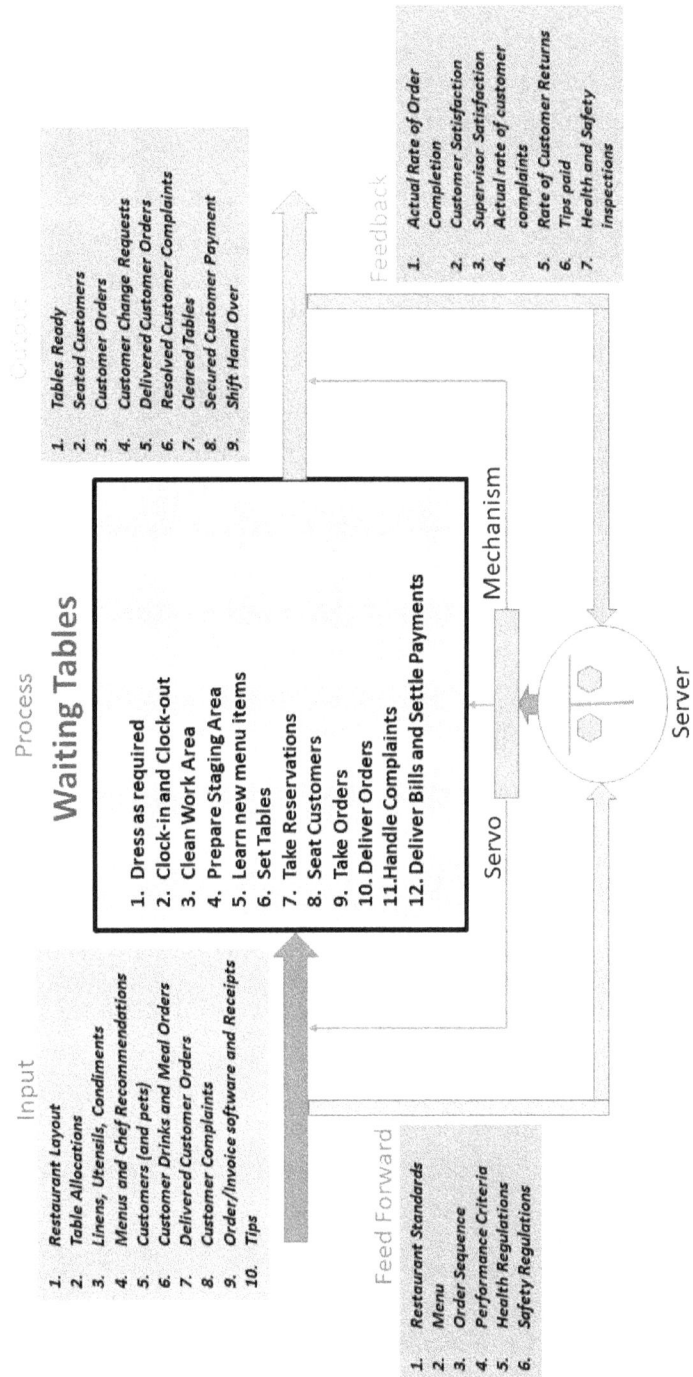

Figure 17 Complete Systems Diagram for a Server in a Restaurant

Read the list of Feedback mechanisms first and then read the Feed Forward standards provided.

Restaurant Server – INs and OUTs with Controls

As we see in Figure 17, in the case of the Server in a restaurant, there are no gauges or meters that provide either Feed Forward or Feedback. The Server must rely on visual cues and timing like:

- The rate of order completion (on time or slower than the required preparation standards)
- Customer satisfaction (in the form of comments or responses to the Server's questions)
- Rate of customer complaints (the percentage of customers returning to the restaurant)

Of course, if the restaurant does not publish a set of standards, there is no Feed Forward by which the Server can 'navigate'. There should be an expectation of how quickly different meals should be completed and ready to serve. There should be a goal for the percentage of customers who come back - otherwise how does one know if the restaurant is really providing exceptional taste and an excellent customer experience? We favor this illustrative format for Job Descriptions in an organization rather than the long, text-based documents that are typical in most companies.

Having done the high level INs and OUTs analysis and having confirmed all the processes and controls in the job, Researchers are now in a position to do an INs and OUTs analysis for each of the process steps listed in the Process Flow Chart. For example, let's take the process steps for "Table Settings," Figure 18. The Output is a table set correctly and ready for use. The inputs are the Server's table allocations, linens, utensils, condiments, menus and the list of chef's recommendations. The Process box contains the list of tasks. Note the Feed Forward section. The photograph (Figure 9) of the required Table Setting from the Internal Environment analysis can now be used as one of the Feed Forward standards. Note the measures of successful performance.

The number of INs and OUTs captures will depend on the number of processes in the Process Flow. The 7 Steps application will generate a Checklist for each of the INs and OUTs created by an occupation Researcher. Checklists are a huge benefit for the organization's Talent Development specialists who can use the Checklist to provide the content for drafting a script for a video/virtual reality or PowerPoint-type sequence teaching exactly how each step should be performed.

The INs and OUTs content is typically compiled by watching the task being performed and writing down the steps. These days, Talent Developers usually capture and analyze the task using video cameras or a smart phone. These sequences are then uploaded into the 7 Step application in the INs and OUTs page for a researched process and then converted into Checklists that can be viewed by other employees on the job, on-demand, from the 7 Step smartphone/smartpad app. (See Page 62vb.)

When Researchers capture the sequence of steps in a process, as someone proficient in the job tells it to them, they should always return for a later interview and check that they've captured the tasks correctly in the best sequence. A review of the INs and OUTs page is the best place to identify needed corrections or changes.

Set Tables

Input

1. *Restaurant Layout*
2. *Table Allocations*
3. *Linens, Utensils, Condiments*
4. *Menus and Chef Recommendations*

Feed Forward

1. *Number of Placements in Territory*
2. *Restaurant Standards*
3. *Required Layout Pattern*

1. Inspect tables in assigned territory to ensure table and floor are clean and ready
2. Count chairs per assigned table
3. Note total seating placements
4. Select large tray
5. Select total napkins, utensils and tumblers to match total placements
6. Select total linens and condiments for total tables
7. Place table linen evenly per assigned table
8. Step back to check even placement
9. Place napkins, utensils, tumblers evenly on each table
10. Place condiments in table center
11. Step back to check even placement
12. Repeat as necessary.

Output

1. *Tables Ready*

Feedback

1. *Zero Customer Complaints about Setting*
2. *Supervisor Satisfaction*
3. *Actual rate of Customer Complaints*

Mechanism

Servo

Server

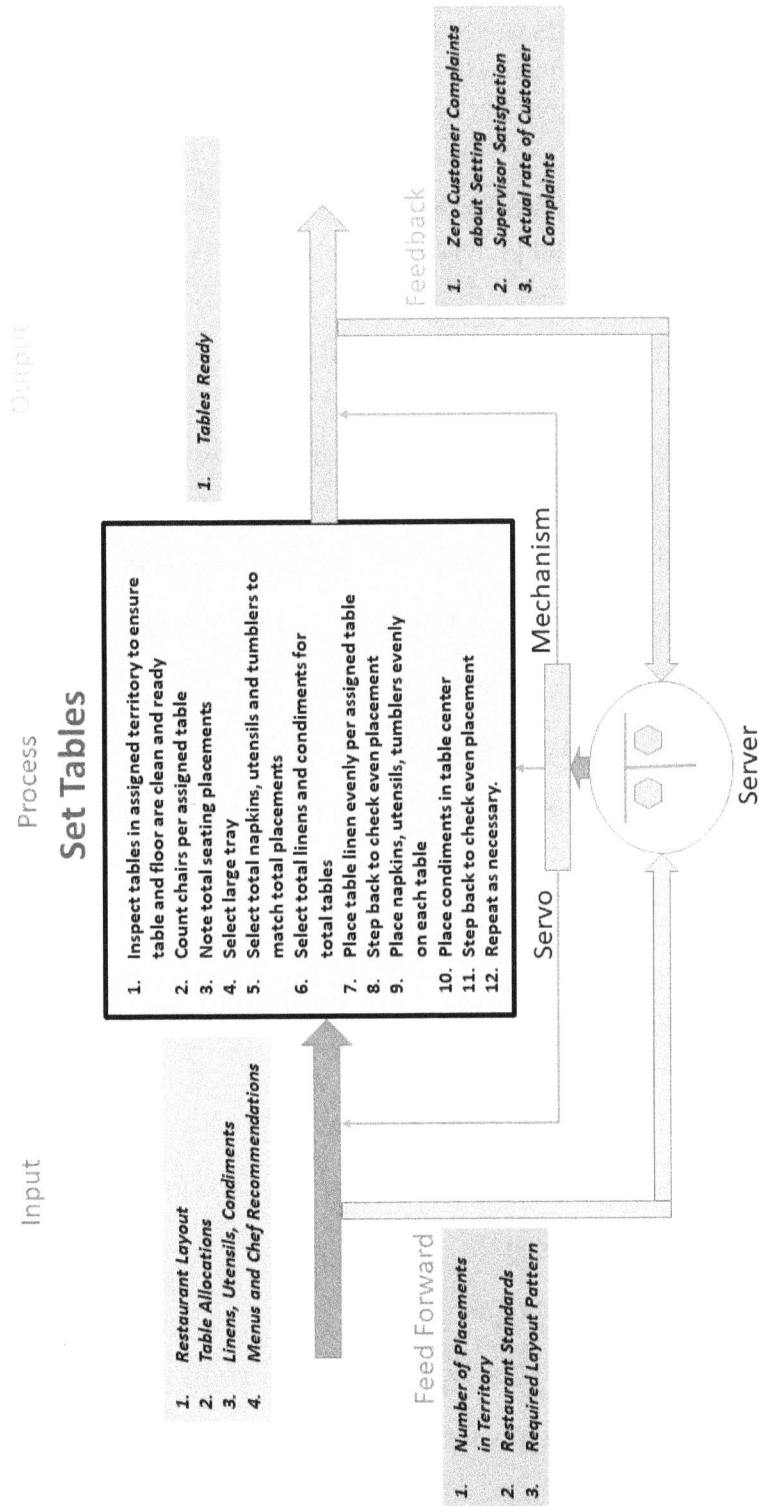

Figure 18 Complete Systems Diagram for Setting Tables

Here is where the In-Company Mentor, department supervisors and managers get opportunities to make improvements in how the tasks **should be performed**. Usually, project participants are not aware of how to make improvements the first time they create the INs and OUTs page. The more times they perform the task, the more likely they are to think up better ways to do it. Researchers should not assume that the way they're first shown the task is the only way or best practices way to execute the steps.

As the team thinks up better ways of doing things, Researchers should take time to come back and update their INs and OUTs charts and generate fresh Checklists for the benefit of employees using the content.

'Things to Do' and 'Questions to Ask' to List "Outs", "Ins", "Processes", and "Controls"

Things to Do

- Begin by trying to document an INs and OUTs **overview** of the **whole** job – rather like a job description in diagrammatic form.

- Start with the blank 'INs and OUTs' capture page in the 7 Steps application.

- Capture a list of the job's outputs first, then

- Capture a list of the job's inputs, then

- Capture a list of the required processes

- Repeat this process for each of the steps in the Process Flow Chart

'Questions to Ask'

In-Company Mentors should warn Researchers that if they just ask their interviewee to list the INs and OUTs of the job, interviewees typically go blank when they see the INs and OUTs capture diagram. On completion of each capture, ask:

- So, when I do the job, what results (**outputs**) will I produce?

- Does it look to you that I've listed the "Outputs" from the job correctly?

- Is there anything that I've missed?

- What are the "Inputs" required to do the job?

- (For each process in the Process Flow) What are the steps required to perform the job?

- Are these in the most logical sequence?

- Have we included 'Best Practices'?

- Let's take one process line at a time, to confirm we've captures all the **inputs** needed to perform that task? (Repeat the question for each listed step in the 'Process' box.)

- So how will I know that I am producing what I should in the right time and quality? What measurement or tracking standards are there?

- What feedback will I get to ensure that I am using the right inputs and processes to produce the required outputs?

- How will I know that I am performing correctly? What standards, specifications, work orders, signs or notices exist that tell me:

    o At what rate I should work?

    o What production quantities I must produce?

    o What quality standards must be met?

    o What safety standards must be complied with?

Checklists

The 7 Step application will generate a Checklist for each INs and OUTs chart captured.

So far the Researcher has used the 7 Step application to complete four job capture processes in the 7 Steps:

1. Internal Environment Chart

2. External Environment Chart

3. Process Flow Chart

4. INS and OUTs Chart – top level view and one for each of the processes in the Process Flow.

CHAPTER 6   FREQUENCIES IN THE JOB

Step 4: Analyze the frequency of tasks in the job. Every job has processes and tasks that occur with different frequencies. Some tasks must be performed much more often than others.

The Process Flow for a job helps the employee identify all the main **processes** they'll be required to perform in the job. In a complex job, this could involve capturing many INs and OUT charts. Some activities in the job are performed far more frequently than others. Some materials or components are used far more than others.

The Pareto Principle

In the introduction to the 7 Steps at the beginning of this book, we introduced you to Pareto's 20/80 principle (Figure 19):

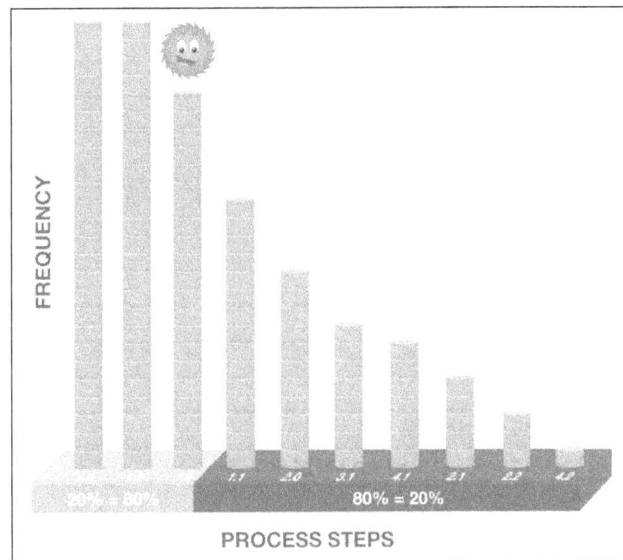

Figure 19 Simple Illustration of the Pareto 20/80 Principle

While, in practice, this is not a guaranteed rule, and there may be small variations one way or the other, you'll generally find that 20% of all the tasks in a job will be performed about 80% of the time. 20% of all the output/products will be produced 80% of the time. 20% of the materials and parts you will use will be used 80% of the time. So, 20% of the parts and supplies required to perform the job will be needed 80% of the time and 20% of all the paperwork, documents and software pages will be used 80% of the time – and so on.

Frequency Analysis for a Table Server at a Retaurant		
Category	Item	Frequency
Processes	Clean assigned area - Usually Bus Boy	C
	Prepare staging area - Usually Kitchen Staff	C
	Learn new menu items - When changed only	B
	Take reservations - Usually Greeters	C
	Set Tables	A
	Seat Customers - Usually Greeters	C
	Take Orders	A
	Change Orders - Lower frequency	B
	Handle Complaints - Lower frequency	B
	Deliver Orders - Usually Kitchen Staff	C
	Process Payments	A
	A's = 3 out of 11	27.3%
		Frequency
Inputs	Tableware	B
	Adult customers	A
	Veagan/Vegetarian customers	C
	Celebration (birthday) customers	B
	Teenage-only customers	C
	Chidren customers	B
	Infant customers	B
	High Chairs	C
	Booster Seats	C
	Wine List	B
	Menus	A
	Serve alcoholic drinks	C
	Beverages	B
	Children's drinks	C
	Bowls for Petfood and water	C
	Meal bill	A
	Credit Cards	A
	Cash	B
	Check	B
	Receipts	A
	A's = 4 out of 20	20.0%
Outputs	Meals delivered correctly	B
	Complaints handled appropriately	C
	Payments processed correctly	A
	Satisfied customers	B
	Tip received	C
	Unhappy customers	C
	A's = 1 out of six	16.7%

Figure 20 Example of listing tasks and then applying the A-B-C Analysis

Things to Do and Questions to Ask Exploring Frequencies in Job Content

Things to Do

- As you capture the Outputs, Inputs, and Processes and key them into the INs and OUTs charts, ask your subject experts to classify them as: A = High frequency, B = Medium frequency or C = Low frequency. (See Figure 20.)

- When you complete the initial capturing, run through the captured content again with a different job expert to confirm the correct allocation of A's, B's and C's.

Questions to Ask

- Which of the Outputs from the job do I produce most of the time?

- Which of the raw materials will I handle most of the time?

- Which of the supplies and parts will I require most of the time?

- Which of the tools, fittings, appliances, and facilities will I use most of the time?

- Who are the people I'll interact with most of the time?

- Which of the processes will I be required to perform most of the time?

- Please help me assign As, Bs and Cs to these things so that I can see the differences in frequencies.

CHAPTER 7   CHECKLISTS

Step 5: Generate checklists for critical processes. Every job needs one or more checklists to ensure that the correct steps and actions will be performed in the right sequence, to the required quality, at the required cost and within all safety requirements.

No one understands the value of Checklists better than people in the aerospace industry do. Pilots never fly without them. The astronaut's support team and every astronaut live by them. There may be a need for a number of Checklists in a job – especially for those processes that are difficult to execute, or which may be critical to safety, quality or costs.

By now, project participants should have a clear picture of the job's Environments, Process Flow, 'INs and OUTs' and Frequencies. They should already have a better understanding of the 'Controls' needed for those processes.

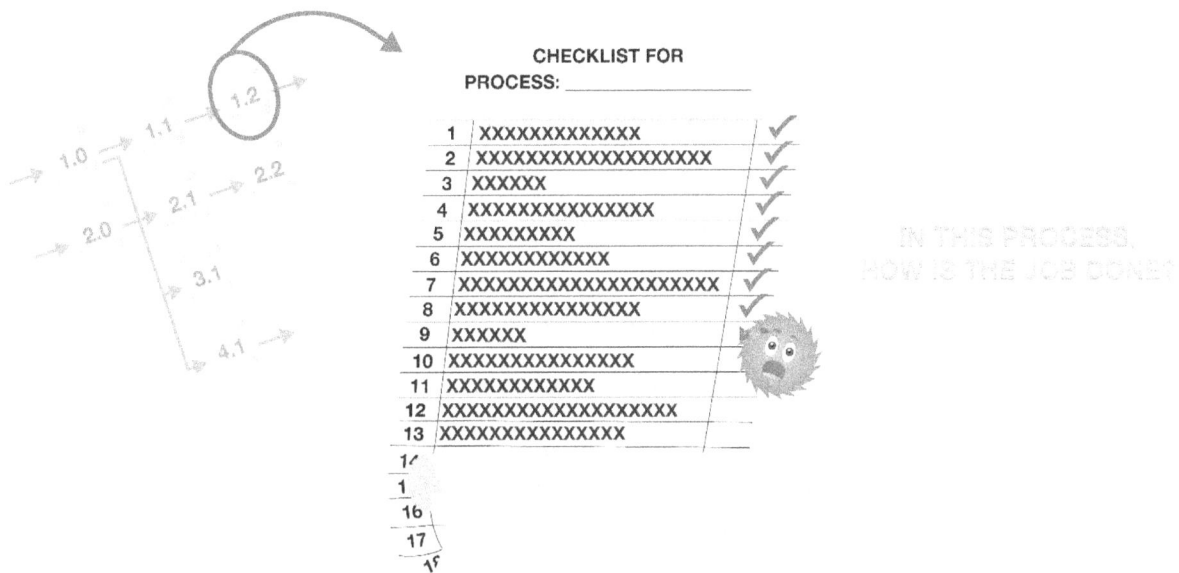

Figure 21 For each Process, generate a Checklist for the Tasks

The 7 Steps application automatically generates a Checklist for each INs and OUTs chart captured. In-Company Mentors should now encourage project participants to sit with someone who really knows each step in the Process Flow well.

Review each checklist to confirm:

- All items and steps have been listed in the most logical and Best Practices sequence
- Identify anything that was missed and needs to be included
- Identify anything that needs to be corrected, or edited out
- Make the **edits in the INs and OUTs chart** from which the Checklist has been generated.

	Restaurant Server Checklist 5: Set Tables
1	Inspect tables in the assigned territory to ensure table and floor are clean and ready.
2	Count chairs per assigned table. Ensure correct.
3	Note and count the total seating placements in the territory.
4	Select a large tray.
5	Select the required total number of napkins, utensils and glasses to match the total required placements.
6	Select the required total number of table cloths and condiments for each table in the assigned territory.
7	Place table linen evenly per assigned table.
8	Step back to check even placement. Correct if necessary.
9	Place napkins, utensils and glasses on table in accordance with the standard table layout.
10	Place condiments in table center in accordance with the standard table layout.
11	Step back to check everything is evenly placed in accordance with the standard table layout. Correct if necessary.
12	Repeat for each table in the territory.

Figure 22 Example of a Checklist for a Restaurant Server

Once 7 Steps has generated the Checklists and the content of the job is made available for viewing, an employee can download the 7 Steps viewing 'app' from the Apple Store or Google Play so that Checklist content and any associated video footage, documents, instructions, etc., can be viewed from a smartphone or smartpad. (See page 62.)

Things to Do and Questions to ask to review Checklists

Things to Do

- View the Checklist generated by the 7 Steps application from the INs and OUTs. (Figure 23)

- Go back and make any necessary changes, corrections, additions, or deletions in the corresponding INs and OUTs chart. (Not the Checklist.)

- Review each Checklist with the assigned job content specialists.

- Review the Checklist with other specialists in the job such as the departmental supervisor and manager, and someone familiar with the job in Safety, Quality Control, Engineering, Operations, OSHA, Union Representative, etc.

Questions to Ask

- Have we listed the items and process steps in the correct 'Best Practices' sequence?

- Is there a better way to do this? Is there **anyone** we can ask to help design improvements?

- Have we captured the correct images, pictures, signs, documents and video clips to illustrate each step for a learner? What else need we capture?

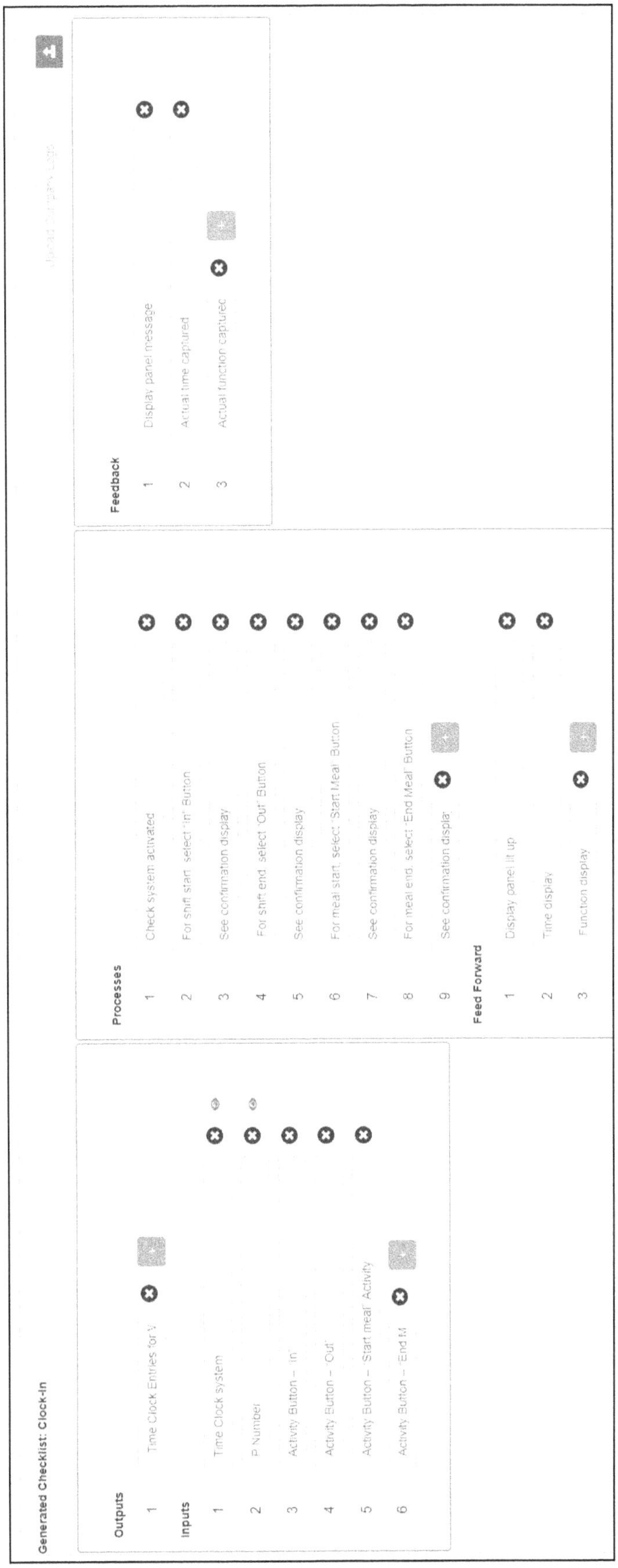

Generated Checklist: Clock-In

Outputs

1. Time Clock Entries for V...

Inputs

1. Time Clock System
2. P Number
3. Activity Button – In
4. Activity Button – Out
5. Activity Button – Start meal Activity
6. Activity Button – End M...

Processes

1. Check system activated
2. For shift start, select 'In' Button
3. See confirmation display
4. For shift end, select 'Out' Button
5. See confirmation display
6. For meal start, select 'Start Meal Button
7. See confirmation display
8. For meal end, select 'End Meal' Button
9. See confirmation displa...

Feed Forward

1. Display panel lit up
2. Time display
3. Function display

Feedback

1. Display panel message
2. Actual time captured
3. Actual function captured

Figure 23 Checklist generated from INs and OUTs

CHAPTER 8   FAULTS

FAULTS

Step 6: Compile a list of the faults that may occur in the job. In every job, things go wrong. Some things go wrong more often than others do.

Have you ever wondered why recruiters look for people with experience? They are really seeking people who've been in a job long enough for the **low frequency** conditions to have occurred sufficient times. Only people with long tenure in a job have seen the low frequency events sufficient times for them to recognize the operating conditions or fault conditions and know how handle them. Training in fault identification and correction should be a critical part of every job entrant's orientation. It surprises us that so many trainers don't include this when providing learning experiences for job entrants.

You'd think that by asking an experienced person to list what can go wrong in a job, they'd be able to help you develop a fault list easily. This is often not the case. Most experienced operators have learned over time to resolve fault conditions as they occur randomly on the job. Faults become blended-in to how they do the job. They typically don't think of faults 'outside of the process box'. Also, when you ask them to list possible faults, they don't typically remember the faults that occur with low frequency. Our experience is that a seasoned person may list only a few faults for you while leaving out many of the faults that can occur. So as project participants proceed in analyzing faults in a job, they'll find things going wrong in a job that they were not warned about. It will be up to them to capture the circumstances and document the conditions of faults that they encounter as they happen. Project Participants need constantly to update their Fault Charts.

Think about things that may go wrong with your automobile. There is typically **more** than **one** cause of a particular fault. Like human illnesses, every fault condition has recognizable **symptoms**. These symptoms are clues to determine the **actual** fault condition that one needs to avoid or fix.

Key Elements in Fault Identification and Correction

Fault Analysis
The Fault Analysis that Project Participants compile should:

- **Identify the fault** using the common name used by everyone associated with the job

- List the **symptoms** that lead an employee to determine possible causes of each fault

- List all the **possible causes** of the fault in such a way that an employee can pinpoint the **actual cause** of the fault

- List the **corrective action** for each **fault cause** to prevent the fault from developing into a safety, quality or cost disaster.

Fault Frequencies

Of course, employees need to initially practice and perfect their ability to apply corrective action to at least the 20% of faults that typically will happen 80% of the time. We recommend that Researchers also establish which of the low frequency faults may cause a serious safety, quality, or cost problem. This may expand the list of initial faults to more than 20% but, in practice we find it is typically less than 30%. It's important that employees practice and perfect their ability to apply corrective action to these critical low frequency faults as well.

Fault Details Capture

The 7 Step application provides a window to capture all the elements above (Figure 24):

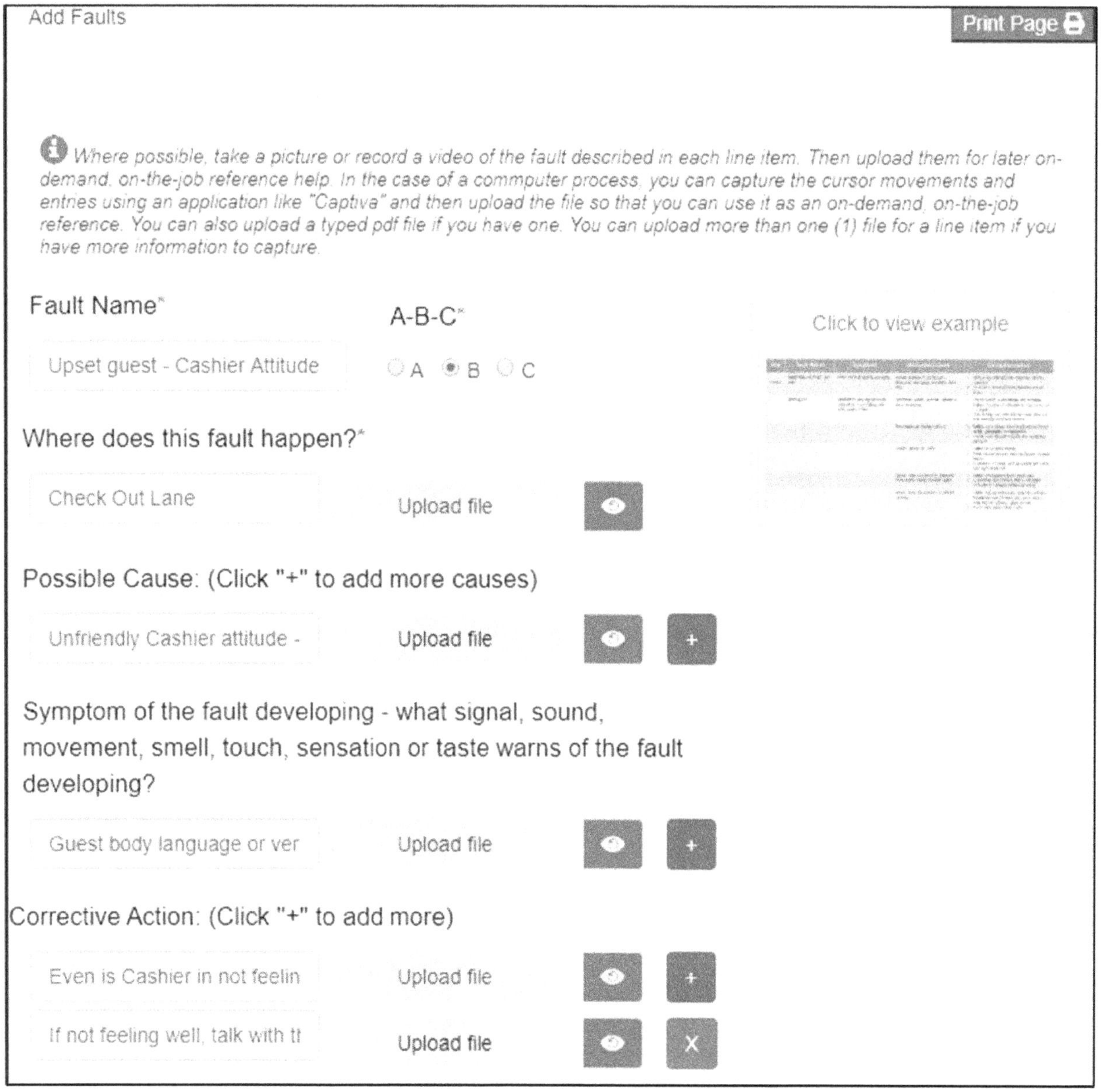

Figure 24 Fault Capture Window in 7 Steps

Fault Diagnosis and Correction Display Layout

The 7 Steps application takes the captured faults content and displays it in a quick reference format.

RESTAURANT MANAGER'S BEST GUESS OF FAULT FREQUENCIES AS "QUANTITIES"

FAULT	PER MONTH	SYMPTOM	POSSIBLE CAUSES	CORRECTIVE ACTION
DISORGANIZED STAGING AREA	4	Plates, utensils, condiments not in the correct positions	1. Busser failed to store items at end of previous shift. 2. Server/manager did not check area before closing.	1. Manager to discipline Busser. 2. Repack staging area at start of new shift. 3. Server and manager to make a point of checking the area before shift closing.
PLATES, UTENSILS, ECT MISSING	4	Lower than normal levels of utensils in cupboards	1. Wash machine not cleared after drying cycle. 2. Wash machine loaded late and still washing. 3. Server/Manager did not check Staging Area before closing.	1. Clear wash machine at start of shift and repack cupboards. 2. Busser to check washer and cupboards before closing. 3. Server/Manager to check staging area before shift closing.
ITEMS MISSING FROM TABLE SETTINGS	18	1. Missing items identified on Server's first patrol of territory 2. Customer complaints	1. Server did not perform a patrol at the start of shift. 2. Server forgot to place the items noticed as missing during a patrol.	1. Manager to check that Server performs the standard patrol pattern at start of shift. 2. Manager to assist by placing the missing items correctly. 3. Manager to discipline Server for not performing inspection patrols.
INCORRECT TABLE SETTING LAYOUT	4	Utensils, condiments, etc. in the wrong positions	1. Server ignored the required standard layout. 2. Table was set by an untrained Server or Busser.	1. Manager to perform own patrol pattern to identify any errors. 2. Manager to retrain Server or discipline Server (if a frequent occurrence) 3. Manager to identify who set the tables incorrectly and train them
CUSTOMERS SEATED INCORRECTLY AT A 'RESERVED' TABLE	4	Customer with the reservation complains when required to wait for next table availability	1. Greeter made mistake when seating non reserved customers. 2. Customers sat themselves at the wrong table and refuse to move. 3. Customer with reservation arrived late.	1. Manager to discipline Greeter appropriately. 2. Accept the customer error. Better to have the customer return than inconvenience or anger them so that they never return. Offer customer with reservation an alternative available seating and something free to compensate. 3. Apologize about error caused by late arrival. Offer an alternative available seating and something free to compensate.
INCORRECT DRINKS ORDER DELIVERED	16	Customer complains	1. Bar tender did not understand the Server's order. 2. Bar tender poured the wrong mix. 3. Server captured the drinks order incorrectly. 4. Server delivered the correct order to the wrong table.	1. Bar Tender/Servers to set up a system of calling back the order for Server to ensure that Bar Tender understood correctly. 2. Manager to check on Bar Tender training or motivation. 3. Server to apologize, capture the correct order and offer something free to compensate. 4. Server to apologize, transfer order if not touched, deliver correctly and offer something free to compensate. manager to investigate possible other causes.

Figure 25 Example for Listing Faults in a job and determining frequencies.

These could be expressed as either an A, a B, or a C where an A is classed as a high frequency fault.

In some jobs, for example, manufacturing, processing and transport environments, it's possible to extract statistical reports on the frequencies of different fault conditions. However, in practice, for most occupations, one has to start by relying on observations and opinions of people experienced in the job.

Fault Checklists

A Fault Checklist has a different layout to the Checklist capture format previously shown. The layout reflects the critical elements of fault detection and correction. A Fault Checklist can be laid out in columns headed:

Fault Name   **Symptoms**   **Possible Causes**   **Corrective Action**

We see this in the Fault Checklist, Figure 25, for the Restaurant Server. Note that for most faults, there is more than one possible cause. To keep a job in control, employees must **diagnose** the **correct** cause and **fix that one**.

In a situation where customer interaction and service is involved, it's important to minimize a customer's disappointment quickly, minimize any delays, and resolve the problem to give the customer a good experience despite the temporary fault condition.

Note how the Server should keep looking out for fault conditions occurring and take quick corrective action or immediately call for assistance in handling the problem if it's not one of the Server's 30%-ers.

The 7 Steps 'app' in the Apple Store and Google Play displays both the Checklists and the Fault Diagnosis and Correction procedures for fast viewing on-the-job from a smartphone or smartpad.

Things to Do and Questions to ask to build Fault Checklists

Things to Do

- With the help of a few on-the-job mentors, compile a list of things that can go wrong in the job. (It's wise to ask more than one person with experience in the job. You will find that people struggle to think of the things that go wrong because they become so accustomed to correcting things in the normal flow of the job that they don't think of them as faults. It takes some digging to get a fully representative list.)

Questions to Ask

- In your experience, what kinds of things go wrong in this job?

- What can go wrong with the Outputs produced in this job?

- What can go wrong with the materials or supplies used for this job (Inputs)?

- What can go wrong in applying the process steps?

- What can go wrong in interactions between the employee and customers, other employees, vendors or contractors?

- What can go wrong with the control systems and reporting for this job?

- Which faults happen more than others? (Identify as either A, B or C.)

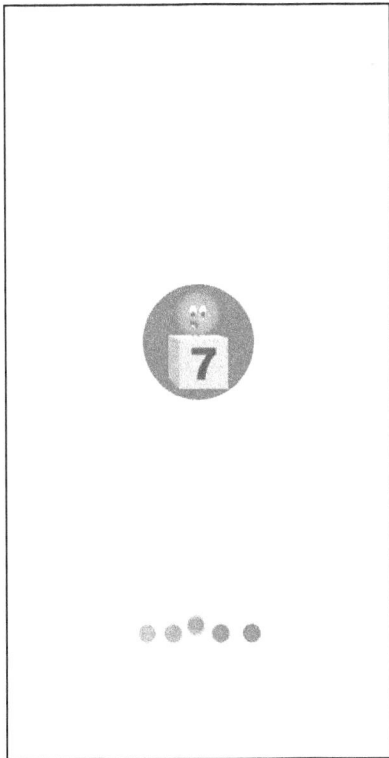

7 Steps App

In

Apple Store

and

Google Play

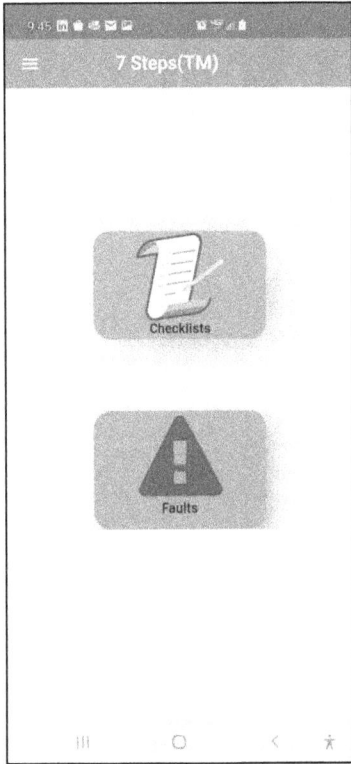

Allows Viewing of Checklists and Fault Diagnoses On-the-Job

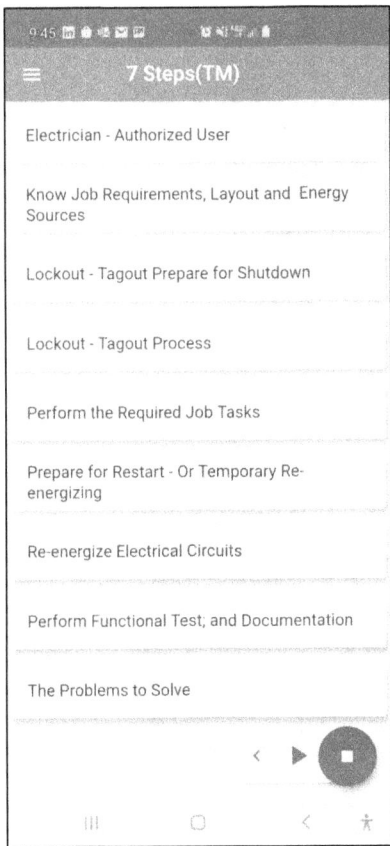

Select the required Checklist from the listed Processes

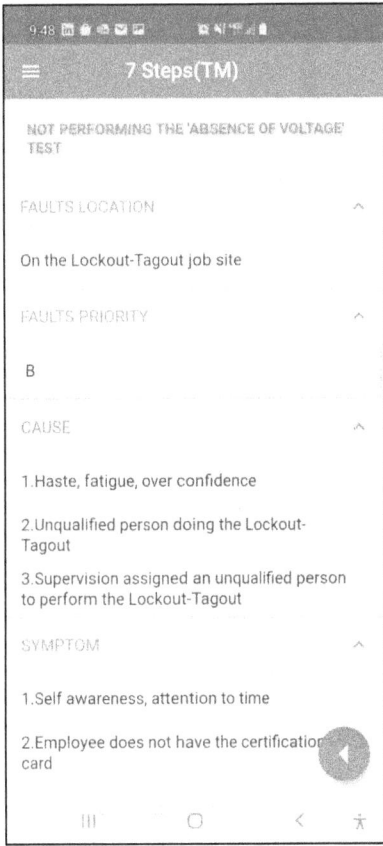

Electrician - Authorized User

Know Job Requirements, Layout and Energy Sources

Lockout - Tagout Prepare for Shutdown

Lockout - Tagout Process

Perform the Required Job Tasks

Prepare for Restart - Or Temporary Re-energizing

Re-energize Electrical Circuits

Perform Functional Test; and Documentation

The Problems to Solve

Touch to get drop-down for the Checklist detailed line items

NOT PERFORMING THE 'ABSENCE OF VOLTAGE' TEST

FAULTS LOCATION

On the Lockout-Tagout job site

FAULTS PRIORITY

B

CAUSE

1. Haste, fatigue, over confidence

2. Unqualified person doing the Lockout-Tagout

3. Supervision assigned an unqualified person to perform the Lockout-Tagout

SYMPTOM

1. Self awareness, attention to time

2. Employee does not have the certification card

Figure 26 Example of a Driver's Eye Patrol Pattern

CHAPTER 9   PATROLLING

Step 7: Develop a Patrol Pattern and Inspection Sequence. Success depends on correct performance in many locations in the job and at many process points.

Successful employees set up a patrol pattern and regularly inspect important elements in the job. By patrolling events in the job, they constantly monitor that things are in control and operating correctly. They also exercise early recognition of the **symptoms** of developing faults, allowing them to take quick corrective action.

We see Patrol Patterns and Inspection Sequences every day all around us, for example:

- Police teams, who patrol our neighborhoods and public places looking for symptoms of developing problems, keep things in control by taking preventive action early.

- Nursing teams in hospitals regularly observe their patients and check their monitoring systems so that they are on-the-spot to take corrective action when they recognize symptoms of developing problems

- Pilots and Air Traffic Controllers have a regular pattern of communicating, reporting and confirming locations and flight conditions to ensure stable flight patterns or to anticipate flight path problems.

Example of a Patrol Pattern When Driving

If you drive a vehicle, you probably already apply a Patrol Pattern and Inspection Sequence – or should! Study the suggested Patrol Pattern in Figure 26. Follow the arrows from 1 through 11:

- The Patrol begins at 1, the road ahead, where the driver observes changing traffic patterns, speed, road signs, illuminated brake lights or traffic signal changes. The eyes then drop briefly to the navigation panel (2) while moving across (3) to the passenger rear view mirror (4). When anticipating a lane change or turn, the driver will not only look at changing traffic patterns behind and the speed of approach of any vehicle but will check the blind spot before changing lane.

- From the rear-view mirror (4) the eyes travel back (5) to the road ahead (6) always checking for changing traffic patterns, changing speeds, road signs, brake lights or traffic signals illuminating.

- From here the eyes lift to the central rear-view mirror (7) once again checking behind for changing traffic patterns, accelerating and approaching vehicles. The eyes drop to the road ahead again (8) and dwell to take in the changing scene ahead.

- From here they move (9) to the driver's side rear view mirror (10) for another look behind. The eyes then move to the instrument panel (11) checking the instruments for speed, engine temperature, and oil pressure while looking for any other alarm lights.

- The patrol then commences again from 1 and keeps repeating itself.

Developing a Patrol Pattern and Inspection Sequence

To be on top of their job, employees need to identify how to use their senses of sight, touch, hearing, taste, smell and rhythm to identify developing fault conditions and **know** that things are in, or out, of control. Employees who have researched the frequencies of faults and have produced a 'Fault Checklist' know what symptoms to look for when they patrol the territory. Many employees aren't taught to think this way and don't develop appropriate inspection patterns for their jobs.

Sensory Elements in a Patrol Pattern

There are different forms of patrol depending on sensory detection in different kinds of job. Here are just a few examples:

- **Movement** around a territory to get to where the action is and where faults are most likely to develop

- **Eye movement** within a territory or a visual scan across a document, computer screen, or monitoring device.

- **Taste detection** - typical in bakeries, restaurants, food production.

- **Smell detection** – typical in restaurants, hospitals, chemical plants, maintenance.

- **Touch detection** – typical in healthcare, maintenance, keyboarding.

- **Sound detection** – typical in entertainment centers, speaker systems, maintenance.

- **Rhythm detection** – vehicle, aircraft, and shipping, engines, musical situations, and professional sport.

Example 1 - Patrol Pattern with Movement

A good Server in a restaurant should have a Patrol Pattern and Inspection Sequence. In fact, one that incorporates all of the sensory elements. In the case of the Server's territory in Figure 27, there are twelve tables to manage. In addition, the Server must keep an eye on 'prepared order availability' in the kitchen and 'drinks readiness' at the bar.

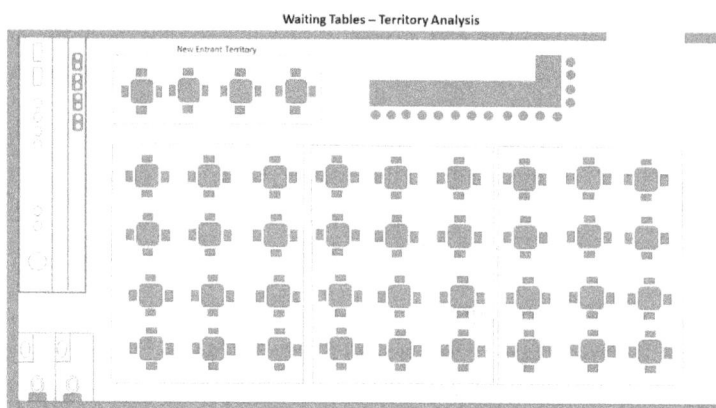

Figure 27 Reminder of the Internal Territory for a Restaurant Server

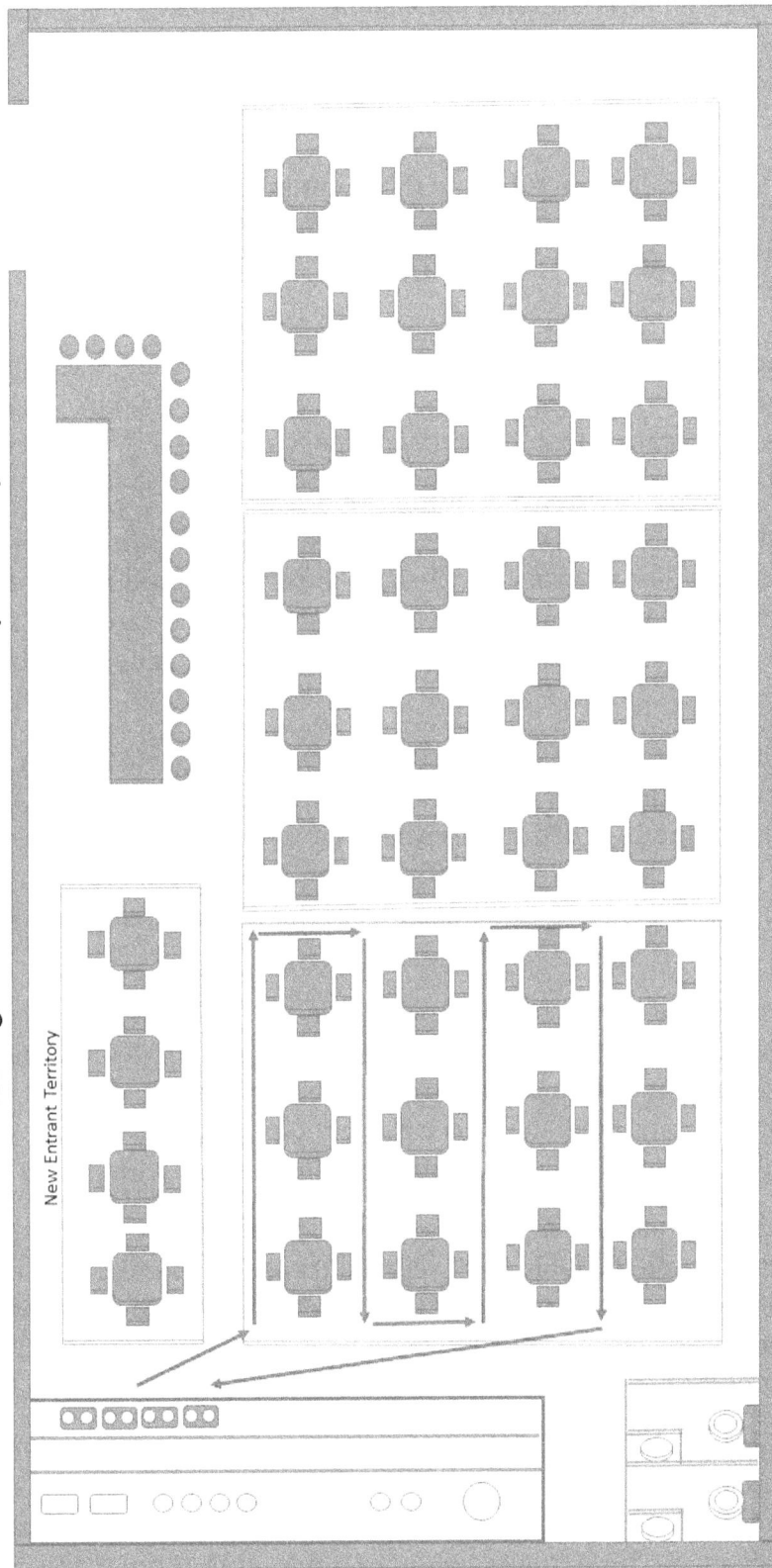

Figure 28 Example of a Patrol Pattern for Restaurant Server

When developing a 'Patrol Pattern – with Movement', the Researcher has to determine the most economic pattern to follow so that employees don't double back and waste time. See Figure 28. This is an example of what the Patrol Pattern and Inspection sequence might be for a Restaurant Server.

The Patrol Pattern doesn't only consist of the direction in which the employee moves, it includes the scanning patterns they use for their eyes and other senses. The Patrol Pattern is a deliberate part of the job. It's like hunting for an enemy. Your senses should be on high alert when you undertake your Patrol Pattern.

The patrol can be interrupted at any time if a fault symptom presents itself or an abnormal event demanding attention occurs. For example, when a Server 'on patrol', hears the executive chef call: "Order 17 Up", the Server, hearing that, and recognizing that Order 17 must be delivered, will divert to the kitchen 'awaiting delivery area' and deliver the food directly to the appropriate diners.

If, while delivering the order, the Server, for example, smells garlic on a plate where the customer had specifically requested that any garlic be 'held', the Server should deliver the rest of the order and apologize to the impacted customer. The customer at the table should be allowed the option of a remake and be delayed while a fresh 'no garlic' meal is prepared or accept the meal if it really does not matter.

The recommended patrol pattern for a Server, when not attending a table, is to start from the 'Food Ready' area of the kitchen. The Server observes the status of the order preparation. If not yet ready, the Server walks towards the assigned territory. As the Server does this, the Server looks across to the bar area to see if any drinks orders are ready. If not, the Server continues to the assigned group of tables. The Server does a broad visual sweep across the whole territory to detect any symptoms of any problem.

As the Server passes each table, the Server looks to the right and visually sweeps the eyes across the floor when approaching each table, looking for any dropped food, personal possessions, napkins, or flatware. The Server then looks carefully at each table to see how the enjoyment of the meal is progressing and to detect any signs of customer dissatisfaction with the meal, drinks or table settings. Servers make a point of asking customers if they need anything else.

The Server repeats this eye-patrol when passing each occupied or unoccupied table to ensure that the 'bussing' staff have cleared the table and prepared it correctly for the next customer. At the end of the circuit, the Server heads back towards the kitchen area still looking towards the right with the eyes sweeping left and right across the whole area again, always anticipating a symptom of developing problems.

At any time that the Server sees food, drinks or any other requirements are ready, the Server breaks the patrol and attends directly to that order. When on patrol, if the Server senses something wrong at a specific table, the Server will break the patrol and head directly to that table. Once the Server has resolved the problem, the Server picks up the patrol from **that** point and continues the circuit.

Example 2 - Patrol Pattern – Close Up

A job often contains elements that must be viewed at close range, for example when processing documents or looking at a landing page in a computer application. (See Figure 29). In such cases, following a special eye pattern allows employees to look at specific places on the page to pick up correct information or to anticipate problems with the information. The eyes travel to those spots where one has to select information to process or confirm. In other instances, employees might be looking in places where faults in document processing typically occur.

How can one expect employees to look for the right things on computer screens, in documents, in reports or in images unless they have been taught the most economic and effective patterns to identify symptoms of faults or to confirm correctness? Some 'experienced' employees get there but only after they have learned the hard way – by omissions or making many mistakes that have to be corrected.

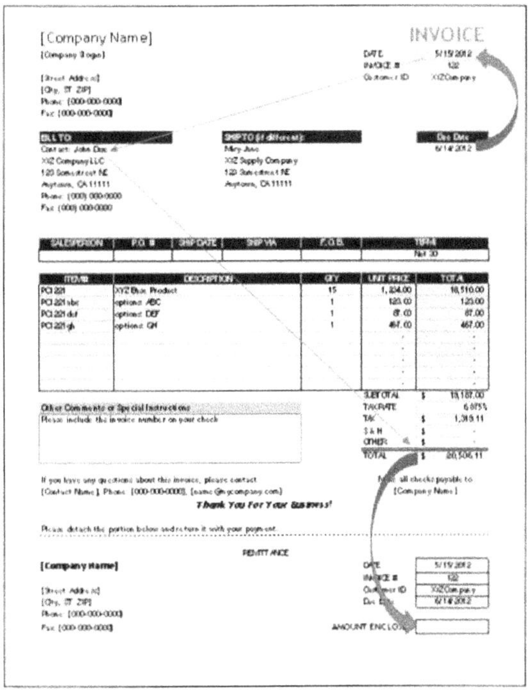

Figure 29 Example of a Patrol Pattern and Inspection Sequence for a Document

Benefits of Different Patrol Patterns

It may seem strange to many employees to think about the need to develop a regular pattern of patrolling the elements in a job and anticipating problems by looking for **symptoms** of developing faults. Remember that early detection and prevention is much better than fixing a problem after the employee has upset the customer or damaged something valuable. No matter how simple or complex the job, there is a rhythm and time frame related to it. The job may require multiple patrol patterns – 'on the move' and 'close up'. A Researcher's diagrams for the different patrols may look different especially in the 'close up' patrols where the job involves different documents and screen layouts.

The 7 Step application helps a Researcher capture as many Patrol Patterns as may be required in an occupation. The Researcher can create a diagram of the area and add the patrol pattern with explanatory call-outs, as seen in Figure 30, or by taking a photograph of the area and adding the patrol pattern with or without call-outs, as in Figure 31.

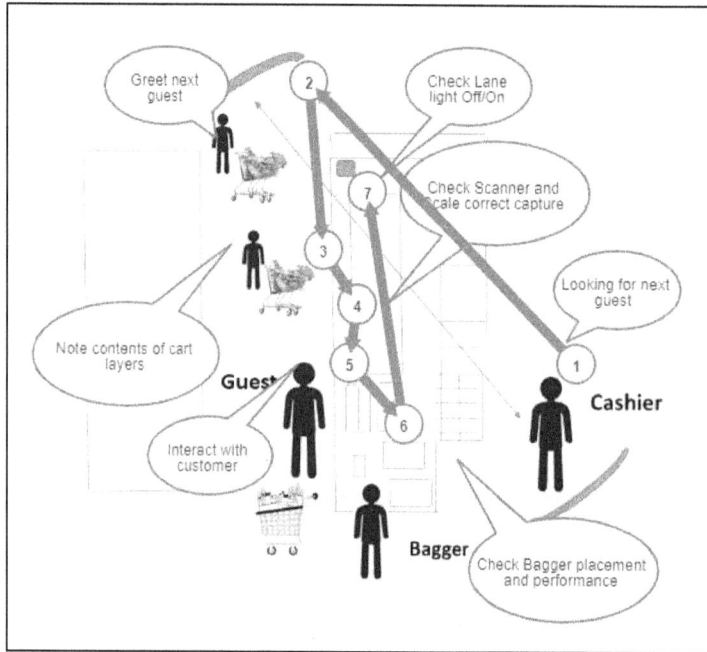

Figure 30 Patrol Pattern Diagram with Callouts

Figure 31 Patrol Pattern over a picture of the work area

As with Checklists and Faults, always be aware of the 20/80 principle. In a patrol pattern, employees should build-in recognition of the fact that some things happen more frequently during the work shift than others. Some happen on a weekly, monthly or even annual basis. If project participants build these elements into their Patrol Pattern diagrams and apply them during their patrolling, they should seldom find themselves in trouble on the job.

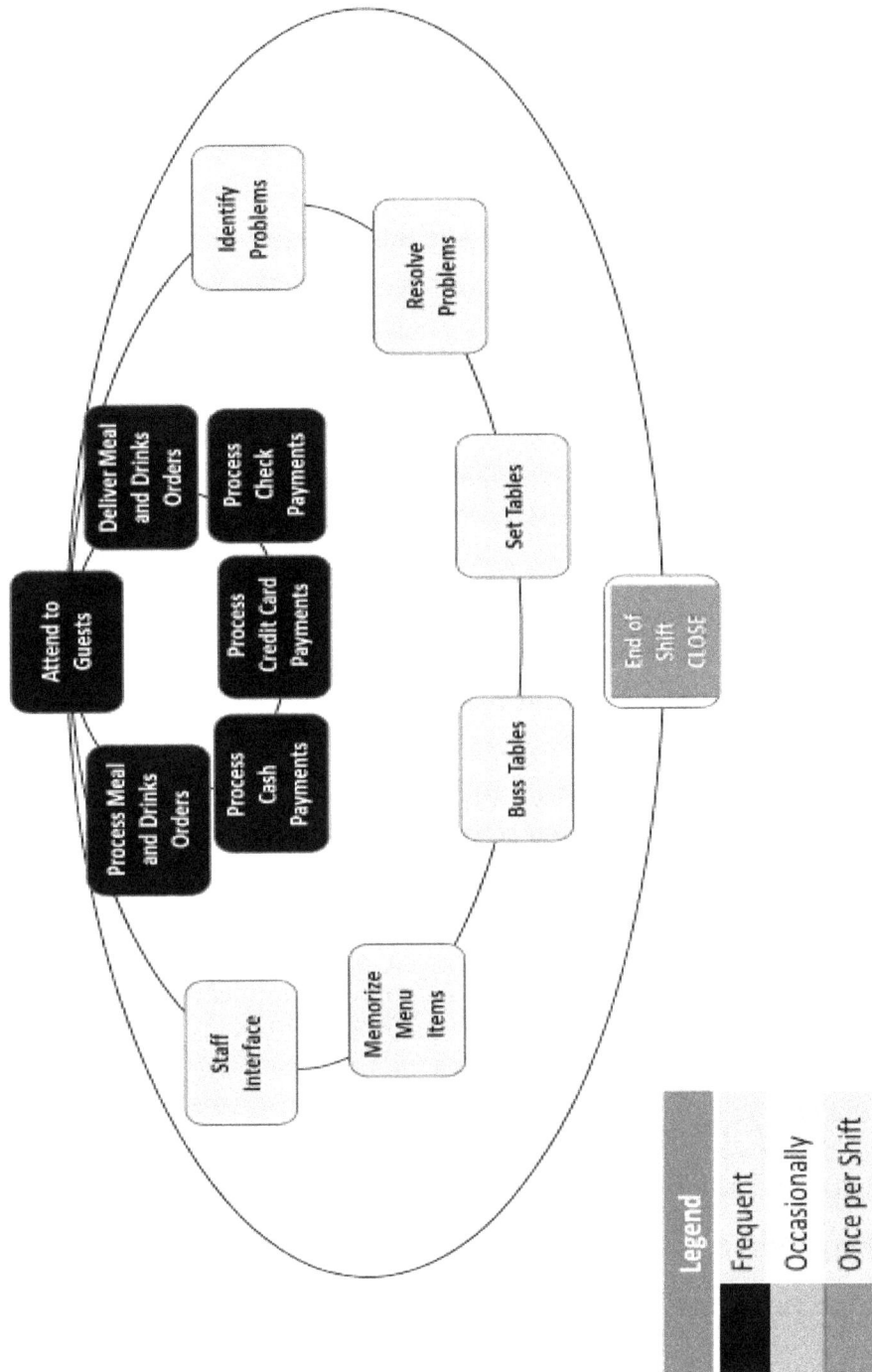

Figure 32 Patrol Pattern Showing Different Frequencies of Inspection

Impact of Frequencies in Developing Your Patrol Pattern

Some things happen more frequently than others. (See Figure 32.) A good Server in a restaurant develops a rhythm for dealing with the multiple tasks that must be performed during a shift. A good Server will sense when the service or tasks are not flowing in a normal pattern. As documents or payments are presented to the customer, a good Server will apply a patrol pattern in scanning the documents or other inputs to review places where information may be wrong. If this isn't done, it may cause a customer to become angry about mischarges on the bill.

Things to Do and Questions to ask to build a Patrol Pattern and Inspection Sequence

Things to Do

- In jobs where there are many people doing the same job, observe the groups in action.
- With the help of a Manager, or Supervisor, identify top performers.
- Observe to see if they have a pattern for patrolling and quality checking.
- Observe how they react when they detect a fault symptom.
- Talk with a top performer and a manager and ask the recommended questions.

Questions to Ask

Remember that you may struggle to get the answers to these questions from your on-the-job mentors. Most job occupants have become so experienced at fixing things that they don't see fault detection and correction as separate actions. Project Participants may have to develop and enhance their versions of the Patrol Pattern and Inspection Sequence as they gain more knowledge of the job:

- In your experience, have you noticed any rhythm, or pattern, for checking-up on things while you're working so that you can detect 'developing problems' early?
- If I wanted to patrol the territory to check that things are in control or to detect the symptoms of a developing problem, what would be the best sequence of inspection I should use?
- When handling a document or a page on a computer application, are there any key places in the document or page for me to check to ensure everything is OK for me to proceed with the task or to determine if I should refer it to someone else first?
- Please don't laugh when I ask you these questions, but:
  - Are there any taste sensations in the job that can warn me of a developing problem?
  - Are there any smells in the job that can warn me of a developing problem?
  - Are there any sounds in the job that can warn me of a developing problem?
  - Are there any touch sensations in the job that can warn of a developing problem?
  - Are there any rhythmic sensations in the job that warn of a developing problem?

So, these then are the 7 Steps that apply to every job. (See Figure 33.) When In-Company Mentors set up projects with selected employees, train them to research, and capture job content from the 7 Step points of view, the company can quickly:

1. Provide employees the information needed to perform the job
2. Provide employees the ability to look-up job checklists and the patrol patterns and inspection sequences on-demand using a smartphone or smartpad – alternatively using a printed manual.
3. Develop video-delivered, secure web-based training programs especially for those jobs with multiple employees doing the same job and especially if they are spread over an extended geographic territory.

In the chapters that follow, we will explore how the 7 Steps have been applied to a collection of positions at different levels in organizations.

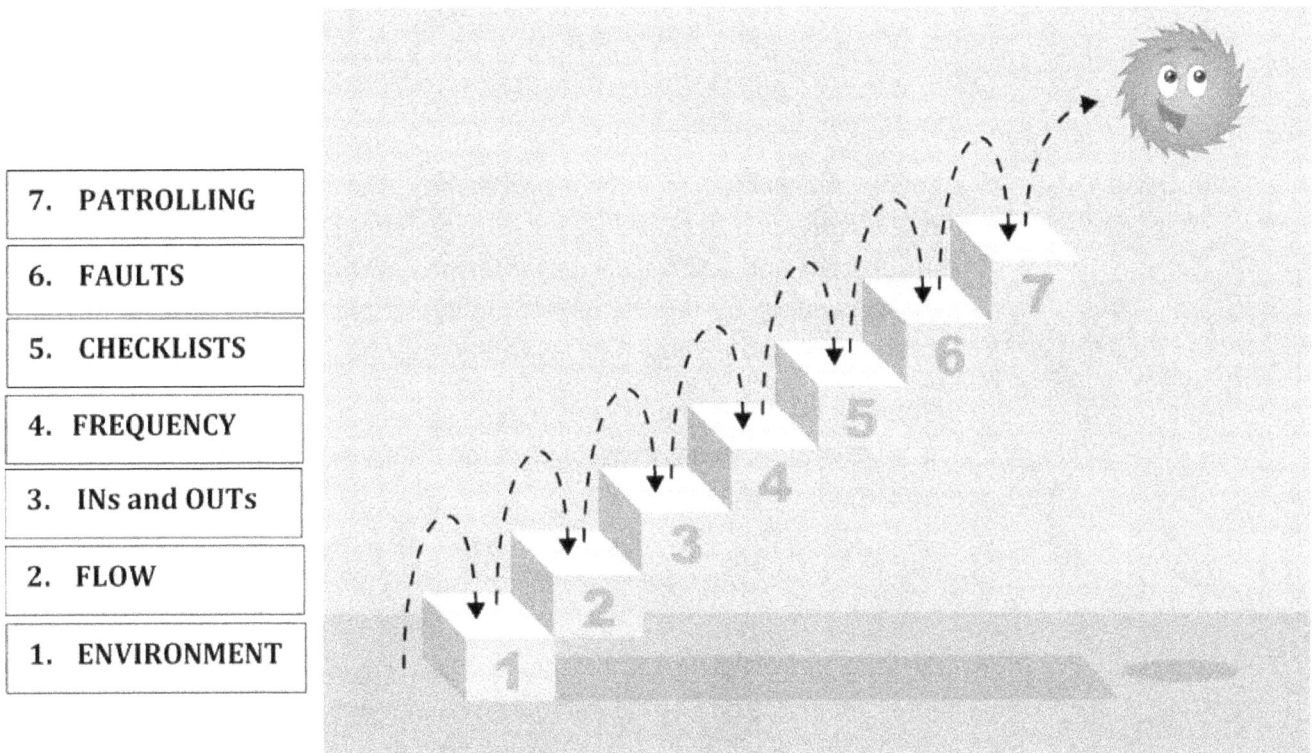

| 7. PATROLLING |
| 6. FAULTS |
| 5. CHECKLISTS |
| 4. FREQUENCY |
| 3. INs and OUTs |
| 2. FLOW |
| 1. ENVIRONMENT |

Figure 33 Layers in the 7 Steps

1	Environment	Define the job's environments. Every job operates within definable environments. You can describe these as *internal* and *external* environments.	ENVIRONMENT
2	Process Flow	Draw the 'flow' in the job. Every job has its own characteristic flow. There is always a point where the tasks start the job cycle and a point where they end it, only to start again. This cycle is the "Process Flow".	PROCESS FLOW
3	INs and OUTs	For each process in the Flow Chart, compile an INs and OUTs diagram. Every job has processes that must be applied to certain inputs to produce specific outputs.	INs AND OUTs
4	Frequency	Analyze the frequency of tasks in the job. Every job has processes and tasks that occur with different frequencies. Some tasks must be performed much more often than others.	FREQUENCY
5	Checklists	Generate checklists for critical processes. Every job needs one or more checklists to ensure that the correct steps and actions will be performed in the right sequence, to the required quality, at the required cost and within all safety requirements.	CHECKLISTS
6	Faults	Compile a list of the faults that may occur in the job. In every job, things go wrong. Some things go wrong more often than others.	FAULTS
7	Patrolling	Develop a Patrol Pattern and Inspection Sequence. Success depends on correct performance in many locations in the job and at many process points.	PATROL

Figure 34 Summary of the 7 Steps recommended and explained in this book.

CHAPTER 10   TIPS FOR YOUR FIRST WEEK ON THE NEW JOB

What if you are a Talent Developer assigned to a new occupation or new employee who wants to use the 7 Step approach to accelerate your onboarding to a new position? What if no job content training is offered in the new department other than sitting by experienced workers and observing what they do?

We recommend that you take the initiative to show that you are a self-starter who can develop something that will not only be beneficial for you but helpful to others in your new department.

Day 1

The first day on the job is usually an orientation day. The Human Resources department, if there is one on site, may provide an Onboarding Session in which you complete the required company documents and participate in a general presentation (or online class) that welcomes you to the organization and outlines company policies and employment practices. These general sessions are seldom specific to your new job. Once you've been signed up for payroll and benefits requirements, you are usually handed over to your new manager and shown to your workstation.

Sadly, in many companies, that's where you might sit for many hours during the first few days. Often there is no one available to start teaching you the elements of the job. Manager's and other workers have to get on with the tasks required in their own jobs. In many instances, you'll be given short bursts of training amidst many interruptions from people needing decisions from your manager.

You can choose to sit and wait patiently - or you can be a self-starter and begin immediately to organize your future.

Things to Do and Questions to Ask in the First Few Days on the New Job

Things to Do

- Take a walk around the territory at least 2-3 times in a shift familiarizing yourself with the layout. This will provide opportunities to practice greeting people by name and start the foundation for the 'On-the-Move' Patrol Pattern and Inspection Sequence you need to develop.
- Introduce yourself to people working in that area. If they have business cards, pick one up from each person. The business cards will provide the correct spelling of their names, and job titles.
- If permitted, take smartphone pictures of other applicable work areas when the people who work there are present.
- Begin creating memory prompts to help you remember faces and names.
- Begin greeting people by name as you arrive at work each day and move around the new territory. If you cannot remember a name, show that you're thinking hard. You'll find most people respond well if they see from your body language that you're trying to remember their name. They might even offer clues that work for them with other people.
- **Begin applying the 7 Steps**

Questions to Ask

- If it applies in your new job, ask your Supervisor to demonstrate the required method for time reporting.
- Ask for a current organization chart for at least the area you'll work in.
- Ask for a current telephone list and get help to highlight the names of the people with whom you must interact on the job.
- Ask if someone in your department can volunteer to walk you around and introduce you to the highlighted people.
- Ask where to get stationery supplies like paper, pens, pencils, erasers, stapler and a binder to assemble the information you collect to capture in the 7 Steps application.
- Ask the location of the restrooms, break rooms and lunchroom (if provided)
- Ask if there are any employment "Do's or Don'ts" that you should know about.
- Ask: "Of the people I have met, who has worked in **this** position before?"
- Ask: "Who do you suggest could be a mentor in teaching me sections of this job?"

(Ease into the last two questions. Pick the appropriate timing so that it doesn't sound like you're unhappy with the limited attention from your manager or assigned trainer.)

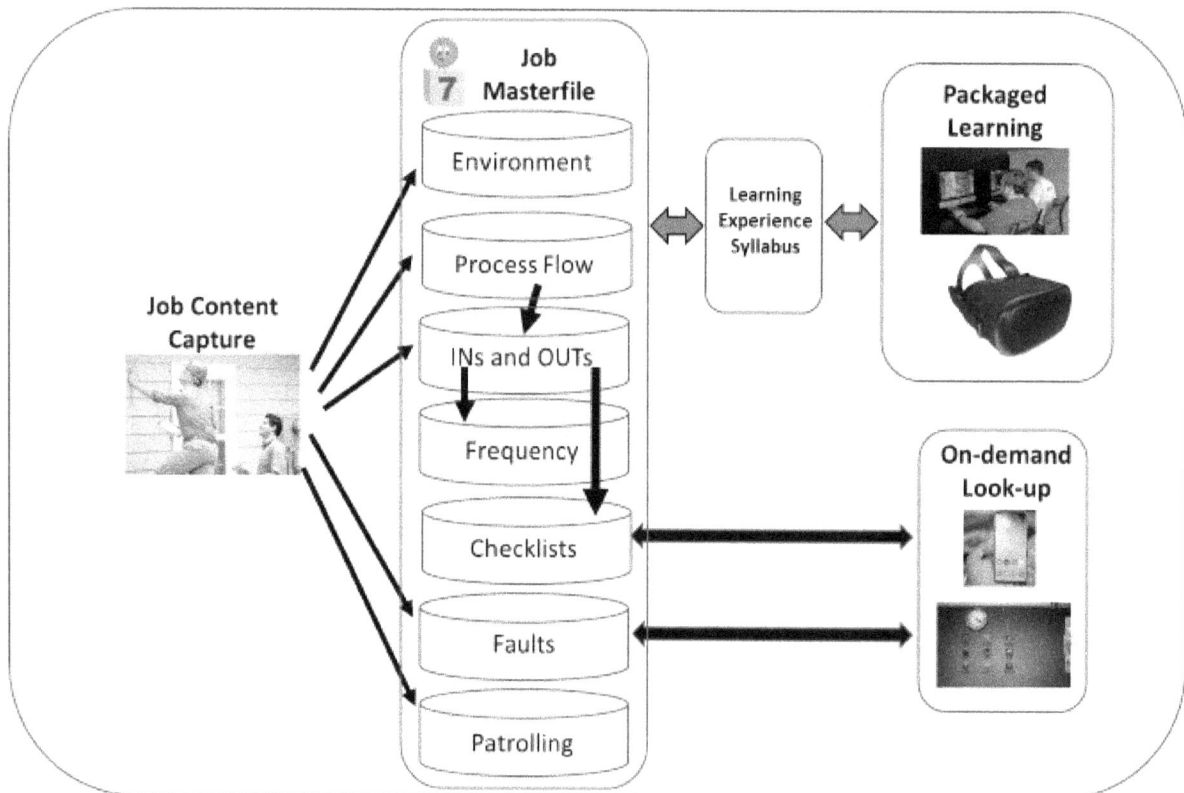

Begin with the first menu option on the 7 Steps Menu Bar, the Job Profile. This allows you to capture the time and people framework of the job. You will capture the names and titles of Managers, Supervisors and work associates. You will capture the job timeframes including start and stop times, break and lunch times etc. You will capture information concerning your payment cycles. Often people forget to tell you these things and you learn them randomly.

By completing the Job Profile, you quickly understand the framework within which you will be required to operate. (See Figures 35 and 36)

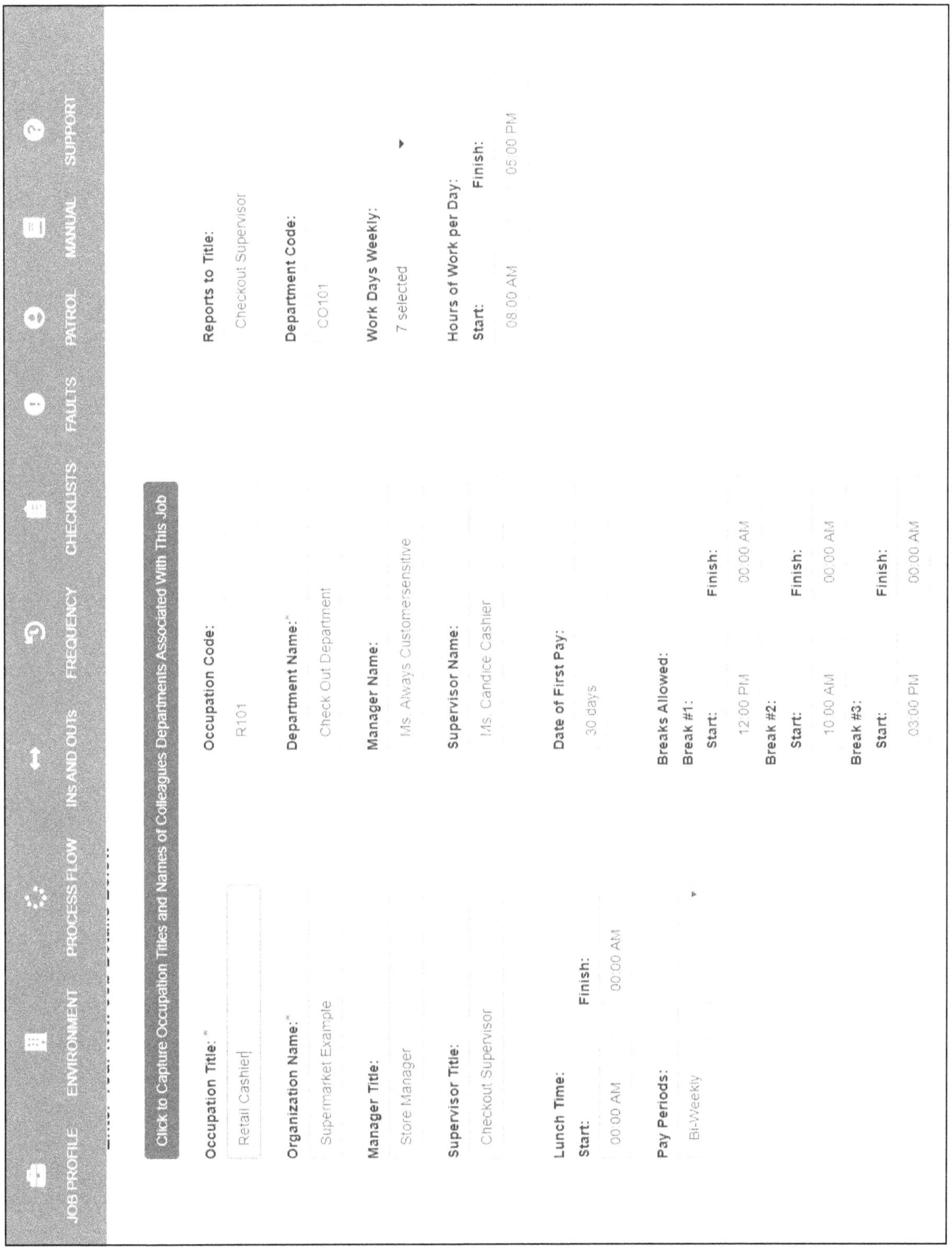

Figure 35 Job Profile Capture Items

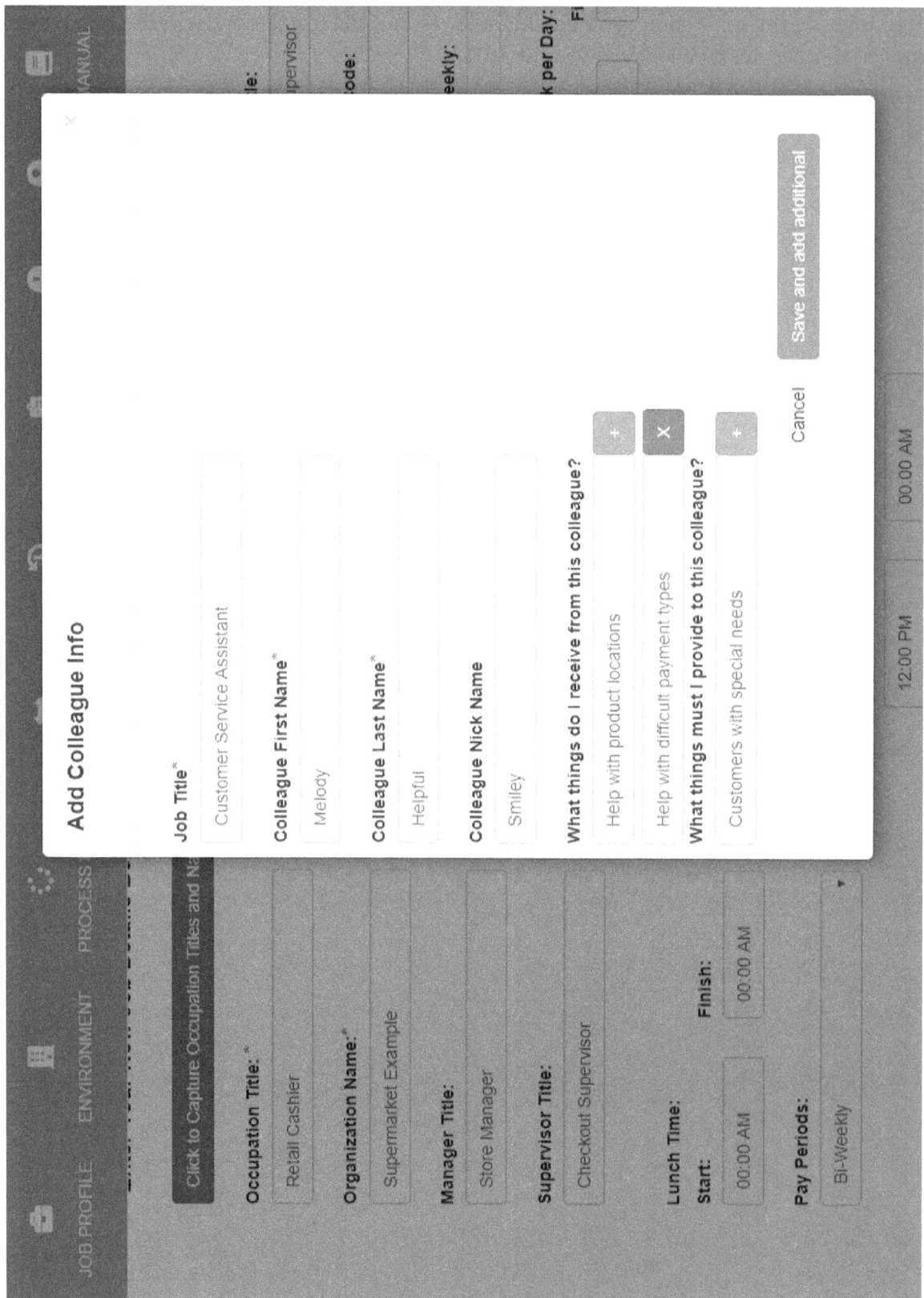

Figure 36 Job Profile - Capture Colleagues

CHAPTER 11   MOVING UP

So there you have it. You're now equipped with **7 Steps** for quickly capturing the content of your new job. Once again, don't expect to be given **all** the information about your job when you start. Sadly, many companies still go no further than providing you with 'onboarding information' that does little more than help manage your payroll and benefits participation. Some corporations do a good job of providing information about the corporation like its history, importance of its brand image, and hints for good customer service. Some major corporations may even go so far as to provide some online education on how to use the online administrative systems. Few companies actually provide enough information about what to **do** in **specific** occupations.

Reaching Out from Day 1

When you wish to enter a new job up the line, it's up to **you** to reach out and get the information you'll need. This is an early test of your motivation, drive and personality. To make a **Fast Start** you need to:

- Identify people with some experience of the new job
- Identify potential mentors
- Reach out to each of the potential mentors
    - Get to know them as people
    - Ask about their families
    - Ask about the job they are doing and how they like it
    - Ask how much experience they have of doing their current job
    - Ask if they would be willing to make time in their workday to spend with you explaining what you must know to perform their job when they get promoted
- Make rough, detailed notes as you talk with mentors
- Use the 7 Steps application to build the job Masterfile
- Update your information regularly.

Build the Job Masterfile

Treat the Job Masterfile as a 'living' creation. In other words, keep updating it as you learn more about the job. As you encounter new documents or signage, upload the document or photos of the signage. If you find that a process, that you thought was **not** critical, turns out to be important, or complex to perform, create an appropriate INs and OUTs capture and generate the Checklist to help you.

Importance of the Job Masterfile

Your Job Masterfile will not only be helpful to you when you need to look up a procedure, Checklist or examples of correctly completed documents, but it will brand you as "someone to be noticed" in the company. The higher the position in your organization, the greater the 'surprise' element will be when others realize that you've created job content that will allow those following you to advance more quickly. Once you get the content of the Masterfile to where it provides an excellent insight into the job, share it with your Supervisor and Manager. Ask them to review it for accuracy and to provide editing and suggestions for improvement.

Most Managers are surprised when presented with such content. In many cases, you'll find that it's the first time a Manager has insight into the complexities of the job. Because it's highly visual with its diagrams, photos, smartphone videos and sample documents, it gives Managers the reassurance that they have 'made a good hiring choice'.

Be careful how you 'present' the 7 Steps content to a Manager or any colleague. Use a 'soft' approach so that people don't perceive you as arrogant and bragging. We recommend that, where a colleague has helped you with a diagram or Checklist, that can later be used by other job entrants in this position, you include their name with yours in 'credit' emails. You gain more by giving others credit than you do by advertising only **your** name.

Use the Masterfile as an opportunity to bring credit to your mentors. Since in most jobs nothing like **your** Job Masterfile exists, the very existence of the manual is important for the department you're in. It'll help you and your Manager to train other new people in the job. There's great value in showing that you recognize and value other people. When you build recognition and opportunity for those around you, you'll quickly become noticed for promotion up the line.

Allow **the Manager** to present your finished work to the Human Resources or Talent Development Departments. Let your Manager share some of the credit. Remember it's the goal of these departments to provide quality orientation and training for productivity improvement and employee satisfaction. You may be helping them start a trend. For example, if a number of people in the organization produced their own job Masterfile using these 7 Steps, the organization will quickly build a digital library of occupation content and learning experiences. For the Talent Development team, more training content would be available in one month than any one Talent Development person could achieve in a few years.

Moving Up to the Next Job

These 7 Steps can also be of value to you if you're ambitious and want to move quickly to higher levels in your organization. Once you become familiar with the company and identify the next job you'd like to master, you should start looking for ways to start the 7 Steps cycle again. Be aware that this needs to be handled very sensitively and delicately. If the current incumbent in that job were to think that you want to get to know their job in order to get them 'fired', you'd create an enemy and block your path to the job.

One approach may be to show the Job Masterfile you developed for your current job to the incumbent of the job you want, and offer to help **them** create a similar manual for **their** job. It's all about 'who will get the credit'. If the current incumbent sees this as an opportunity to be noticed, they'd be happy to provide the information but let you do all the work to create the manual.

Once completed, you **must** allow **that** mentor to get the credit.

If you've not yet seen the movie "Pay it Forward[2]" do yourself a favor and view it as soon as possible.

---

[2] **Pay It Forward** is a 2000 American drama film based on the novel of the same name by Catherine Ryan Hyde. It was directed by Mimi Leder and written by Leslie Dixon. It stars Haley Joel Osment as a boy who launches a goodwill movement, Helen Hunt as his single mother, and Kevin Spacey as his social studies teacher. It shows the value of doing something that will benefit others resulting in them following the pattern and doing good for others going forward.

People who have been Successful Using these 7 Steps

We have assembled this sequence of 7 Steps based on years of experience observing people who have moved into new positions and have been quick to become highly effective and successful.

Richard U worked in the fast food industry as an industrial engineer. He excelled as the Vice President of Operations for one of the largest, nationwide, video rental stores and then was responsible for expanding the world's fastest growing luxury coffee stores into the eastern half of the USA. More recently, Richard has been a leading consultant to many retail organizations. His particular delight these days is showing, based on Pareto's 20/80 principle that 80% of an organization's causes of high cost and lost profits typically comes from 20% of the causes. He is a master of Fault Diagnosis and Correction and a role model for Patrol Pattern and Inspection Sequences.

As a manager, he established a pattern for getting around to all of his stores, together with the respective regional managers. We marveled at the way he would enter each store and begin his patrol. He always looked at the location of the staff members and waited till they gave a great customer greeting. You'd then see his eyes sweep the store noticing every detail from shelf layout to promotional displays. He'd move in a pattern around the store, his eyes scanning each shelf in detail noticing positioning of products and enticing marketing offers. Store Managers welcomed his visits – especially when they achieved his very high standards and received appropriate rewards. When reviewing store and regional reports, Richard had his set pattern of scanning the pages looking for telltale symptoms of developing problems. He rose to the top rapidly. His teams loved him as an executive.

Colette M also started as an engineer. In her early days she got into automotive design and 3-D modelling. She suddenly moved to the world of the Internet when her brother asked her to be the President of a company that provided online education for people wanting to start their own web-based business and needed drop ship suppliers. Soon after starting the job, Colette plotted the Internal and External Environments. She quickly realized that Internet bloggers, in those days, were the backbone of growing Internet businesses. She established a network of "Affiliates" who commanded large blog audiences. Internally she established the people support team and a stunning inventory of marketing support articles, promotions, videos and online video teaching sequences for Affiliates to use and adapt free of charge. Her Patrol Pattern included frequent conference calls with Affiliates both individually and in groups. She further realized that the company needed to be part of the territory of corporations like eBay, Amazon, UPS, FedEx and others. She became a leading speaker at conferences and seminars for the early adopters of web-based selling.

Kevin P is an expert in Product Life Cycle Management today. He began as an engineer teaching how to use 3-D modelling software for product design. He naturally applied the 7 Steps. In particular, he was stimulated by Pareto's 20/80 principle. His team soon realized that in all product design, 20% of the design elements are repeated 80% of the time. The team evolved a concept of 'Engineering Design Templates' and provided consulting services to leading designers to help them set up design templates for their product ranges. Imagine someone designing car seats.

When developing a design template there is a basic framework of lengths and widths for the back and seat of the car. There are different angles for the sides. There are different edges and corner styles.

Starting with a template, a designer can begin by simply making changes to widths, lengths, surfaces etc., to generate 80% of the new design. The designer can do this in minutes and then spend time on making the distinctive finishes of the new product.

The 7 Steps will not only help you be seen to make a fast start in your new job, they'll help you evolve perspectives in the job that can lead to innovation and significant improvements in productivity. We hope you'll have fun developing your skills in applying these steps.

Be Successful

We wish you success in every new venture you undertake!

SUPPLEMENTAL READING

Teaching

- How to Teach Adults by William A. Draves   The Learning Resources Network   www.lern.org
- Advanced Teaching Online (Fourth Edition)   The Learning Resources Network   www.lern.org

Pareto Principle

- Wikipedia
  http://en.wikipedia.org/wiki/Pareto_principle
- Better Explained
  http://betterexplained.com/articles/understanding-the-pareto-principle-the-8020-rule/

Systems Theory

- Do an Internet search for "Scholarly articles for Systems theory in learning"
- Conditions of Learning by Robert M. Gagne - Amazon
- Instructional Technology: Foundations by Robert M. Gagne -   Amazon
- View an interesting video on YouTube: https://www.youtube.com/watch?v=EOIGhyiCwpU
- Principles of Instructional Design by Robert M. Gagne, Walter W. Wager, Katharine Golas and John M. Keller (Jun 15, 2004) - Amazon
- Teaching and media: A systematic approach (2nd Ed.) by Gerlach, V.S. and Ely D.P. Allyn & Bacon
- Technology Competencies Problem-Solving
  http://www.wsfcs.k12.nc.us/cms/lib/NC01001395/Centricity/Domain/1555/3.03_Universal_Systems_Model.pdf

Learning Theory

- Do an Internet Search on "Scholarly articles for learning theory psychology"
- Muirhead, Brent. "Online Education: Innovative and Personal" (December 2004).
  Available online: **http://www.itdl.org/Journal/Dec_04/editor.htm.**
- How E-learning Works   howstuffworks.com
  http://people.howstuffworks.com/elearning2.htm
- The Psychology of Learning and the Art of Teaching   Steven Mintz, Columbia University
  http://www.columbia.edu/cu/tat/pdfs/psych_learning.pdf
- Psychology 101   Dr. Christopher L. Heffner Grand Canyon University
  http://allpsych.com/psychology101/index.html
- The Psychology of Learning   Epic Learning Group
  http://epiclearninggroup.com/us/files/2013/03/WP_the-psychology-of-learning1.pdf
- Social learning theory. Bandura, A. (1977). Englewood Cliffs, NJ: Prentice-Hall - Amazon
- The New Update on Adult Learning Theory: New Directions for Adult and Continuing Education (J-B ACE Single Issue)Paperback – May 8, 2001 by Sharan B. Merriam (Editor) Amazon
- The Adult Learner, Fifth Edition: The Definitive Classic in Adult Education and Human Resource Development (Managing Cultural Differences) Paperback – August 20, 1998 by Malcolm S. Knowles Ph.D. (Author), Elwood F. Holton III Ed. D. (Author), & 1 more - Amazon'

INDICES

"A-B-C" Analysis, 23
7 Steps application, 27, 29, 44, 46, 53, 54, 59
A-B-C, 23, 24, 50
Acknowledgements, 2
Check Lists
   - for selected job processes, 16
checklist, 22, 53
checklists
   - for correct application of a process, 22, 25, 46, 53
Checklists, *60*
Copyright, 1
Environment
   related to where the job is performed, 16, 17, 27, 30, 32, 39
External Environment, 32, 33, 47
Faults
   - that may occur in the job, 16, 23, 57
Feed Forward
   - as in systems control, 20, 41, 44
Feedback
   - as in systems control, 20, 41, 44
flow, 18, 25, 30, 35, 37, 38, 53, 60
Flow
   - related to the job cycle, 16, 18, 19, 39
frequency, 21, 22, 24, 25, 49, 51, 57, 58, 59
Frequency
   - related to most occurring job functions, 16
   related to most occuring job functions, 21, 23
Human Resources
   - for people recruitment and support, 78
In-Company Mentors, 31, 39, 46, 53, 71
inputs
   - to each process, 19, 20, 22, 25, 35, 38, 39, 46, 47, 51, 70
Ins and Outs

   - as used in Systems Analysis, 39, 44, 46, 53
INs and OUTs, 19, 22, 25, 35, 38, 39, 40, 44, 46, 47, 51, 53, 54
   - related to the job processes, 16
Internal Environment, 27, 29, 31, 32, 44, 47
Manual
   - as in Job Manual, 77, 78
mentor
   - as in coach and teach, 30, 33, 78
outputs
   - from each process, 19, 20, 22, 25, 35, 38, 39, 47, 51
Pareto, 21, 23, 49
Pareto Principle, *81*
Patrol
   - as applied to the job, 63, 64, 67, 70
Patrol Pattern and Inspection Sequence, *63*
process
   - as aplied to inputs to produce outputs, 18, 20, 24, 25, 26, 35, 37, 38, 39, 41, 44, 46, 47, 49, 53, 57, 60, 63, 77
   - as applied to inputs to produce outputs, 19, 20
Server
   - as in waiting tables, 27, 39, 44
supervisor
   - as in sub-manager, 77
Talent Development
   - for job training and development, 44, 78
The Blair Witch Project
   - Rob Cowie Producer, 2
Union
   - as in Labor Union, 31, 32
viewing, 13, 23, 54, 60
virtual reality, 14, 15, 44
Wilfredo Pareto
   - 20/80 principle, 21

TABLE OF FIGURES

Figure 1 English Log-in for 7 Steps 10

Figure 2 Multi-Language Log-in for 7 Steps 11

Figure 3 Using the 7 Steps System to best benefit 12

Figure 4 Diagram showing that a *Process* needs *Inputs* to produce *Outputs* 20

Figure 5 Identify the 20% to be performed 80% of the time. 21

Figure 6 Summary of the 7 Steps recommended and explained in this book. 25

Figure 7 The 7 Steps Layers 26

Figure 8 Simple Internal Environment for a Restaurant Server 28

Figure 9 The required table layout (Source: Google Images) 29

Figure 10 Example Supermarket Cashier's Internal Environment 30

Figure 11 Examples of Safety Signs 31

Figure 12 Example of the Supermarket Cashier's External Environment 32

Figure 13 Icon favored when building a Process Flow Diagram 35

Figure 14 Example of a Process Flow Diagram in 7 Steps Masterfile 36

Figure 15 Example of an INs and OUTs analysis for a Supermarket Cashier 40

Figure 16 Illustration of the Engineering Systems Diagram. 42

Figure 17 Complete Systems Diagram for a Server in a Restaurant 43

Figure 18 Complete Systems Diagram for Setting Tables...45

Figure 19 Simple Illustration of the Pareto 20/80 Principle...49

Figure 20 Example of listing tasks and then applying the A-B-C Analysis 50

Figure 21 For each Process, generate a Checklist for the Tasks 53

Figure 22 Example of a Checklist for a Restaurant Server 54

Figure 23 Checklist generated from INs and OUTs 55

Figure 24 Fault Capture Window in 7 Steps..58

Figure 25 Example for Listing Faults in a job and determining frequencies....................................59

Figure 26 Example of a Driver's Eye Patrol Pattern 62

Figure 27 Reminder of the Internal Territory for a Restaurant Server 64

Figure 28 Example of a Patrol Pattern for Restaurant Server 65

Figure 29 Example of a Patrol Pattern and Inspection Sequence for a Document...........................67

Figure 30 Patrol Pattern Diagram with Callouts 68

Figure 31 Patrol Pattern over a picture of the work area...68

Figure 32 Patrol Pattern Showing Different Frequencies of Inspection...69

Figure 33 Layers in the 7 Steps...71

Figure 34 Summary of the 7 Steps recommended and explained in this book. 72

Figure 35 Job Profile Capture Items 75

Figure 36 Job Profile - Capture Colleagues 76

www.ingramcontent.com/pod-product-compliance
Lightning Source LLC
Chambersburg PA
CBHW051418200326
41520CB00023B/7278